# CONTENTS

## SNACKS & APPETIZERS ........................................76



## RICE & GRAINS ........................................86

## VEGAN ........................................................................................97



## DESSERTS ................................................................................... 108

# INTRODUCTION

Frying is a common cooking method; it is quick easy, and tasty. Many restaurants and fast food chains use deep-frying as an economical and quick way to prepare foods. Honestly, everybody likes the taste of popular deep-fried foods such as fish sticks, French fries, chicken nuggets, doughnuts, and so on. Mmm, that is oh so delicious! Fatty foods taste so good! Unfortunately, deep-fried food is not good for your health. Deep fried foods tend to be high in calories and trans- fats, which can have negative effects on your weight and overall health.

However, you don't have to sacrifice flavor when trying to eat healthier and shed a few pounds. You should find another solution. An Air Fryer is a unique kitchen device designed to fry food in a healthy way. The Air Fryer cooks food with super-heated air that is circulated by high-powered fans, delivering that crispy, golden-brown exterior and a moist and tender interior. In other words, hot air is a new oil!

Let's say you want to prepare fish and chips. Instead of soaking your favorite food in a quart of hot cooking oil (which was probably GMO refined and old) in your regular pan, you can cook it with a tablespoon or two of healthy olive oil, and get a crispy, delicious food. Best of all – fried food does not taste like the fat. The Air Fryer cuts calories, not flavor! It makes cooking at home easy, quick, and most importantly – healthy!

## Things to Know Before you Buy an Air Fryer

An Air Fryer is a kitchen appliance that utilizes super-heated air to cook food in a special chamber using the convection mechanism. Technically speaking, a mechanical fan blows heat around the space so the hot air circulates around your food at high speed, cooking evenly from all sides, producing crispy browning results. This is called the Maillard effect. According to Wikipedia "The Maillard reaction (/maɪˈjɑːr/ my-YAR; French: [majaʁ]) is a chemical reaction between amino acids and reducing sugars that gives browned food its distinctive flavor. Seared steaks, pan-fried dumplings, cookies and other kinds of biscuits, bread, toasted marshmallows, and many other foods undergo this reaction. It is named after French chemist Louis-Camille Maillard, who first described it in 1912 while attempting to reproduce biological protein synthesis."

This simple but intelligent machine radiates heat from heating elements and uses rapid air technology to fry roast, and bake your food with less oil. The Air Fryer can also warm your food. You don't have slave over a hot stove since the Air Fryer features an automatic temperature control. Thanks to its convection settings, it produces crispier and more flavorful food than conventional cooking methods.

If you are thinking of cutting down on fat consumption, here is a great solution. Studies have shown that air fried veggies contain up to 80% less fat in comparison to veggies that are deep fried. Just to give you an idea of the calorie content – deep-fried onion rings contain about 411 Calories vs air fried that contain about 176 Calories. Deep-fried Chicken Nuggets = 305 calories vs air fried = 180 Calories.

In order to understand how to use an Air Fryer, it would be good to find out more about the anatomy of this magical device. As we said before, there is the inside i.e. electric-coil heating elements. A specially designed fan distributes the hot air evenly throughout the cooking basket. Then, the Air Fryer has a removable cooking basket with a mesh bottom that is coated with a non-stick material. It is placed in a frying basket drawer, cooking your food in the sealed environment. When it comes to the features of an Air Fryer, it has a Control Dials – Temperature Control Dial and 60 Minute Countdown Timer Dial. You can use the preset time and temperature, or increase and decrease the cooking time and temperature to suit your recipe. Timer and buzzer are amazing features since you do not have to worry about overcooking or undercooking your food.

Air Fryers come with accessories, such as baking dishes, pans, trays, grill pans, skewer racks, and so forth; it will vary from model to model. However, make sure to use pans and racks that are designed to fit into the Air Fryer.

## 10 Air Fryer Tips You Should Know

Although an Air Fryer is easy to use, please follow these tips for getting the most out of your new, fancy device. Once you get into it, crispy and delicious foods are just minutes away!

How to keep the rendered fat drippings from burning? Simply pour a little water into the bottom of the air fryer drawer. In this way, the fat drippings can't reach smoking temperatures.

If you miss the traditional fried food, try melting butter and sprinkling in your favorite herbs and spices to shake things up. Then, you can whip up a healthy avocado mayo and a few drizzles of hot sauce for a custom dip. You can use a tablespoon or two of extra-virgin olive oil and add whatever aromatics you like (garlic, herbs, chili, etc.); the result is veggies with a crisp texture and fewer calories. Win-win!

As for cooking times, always test your food for doneness before removing it from the cooking chamber, even if you are an experienced cook. As for meats and poultry, use a meat thermometer to ensure that meat is cooked thoroughly. As its name implies, our Air Fryer Cooking Guide is intended as a guide only. The quantity and quality of food, as well as its thickness or density, may affect actual cooking time. It is recommended to cook food in smaller batches for the best results. Remove the frying basket drawer halfway through the cooking time to check your food. Most foods need to be shaken or turned over several times during the cooking time.

How to achieve that delicious, crispy surface? Pat your food dry before adding spices and oil. A tablespoon or two of oil should be brushed onto foods; experts recommend using oil sprays or misters with your favorite oil (olive, vegetable, or coconut oil). Avoid aerosol spray cans because they have harsh agents that can damage the coating on Air Fryer baskets.

Although most foods need some oil to help them crisp, there are certain foods that naturally have some fat such as fatty cuts of meat; therefore, you do not have to add extra fat to these foods, but anyway, do not forget to grease the cooking basket.

Allow your food to rest for 5 to 10 seconds before removing them from the cooking basket unless the recipe indicates otherwise.

Most of Air Fryer's manufactures specify that the unit should be preheated. However, it is not necessary every time. Simply set your Air Fryer to the desired temperature and wait for 3 to 5 minutes before putting your food into the cooking basket.

If you want to shake or add ingredients during the cooking cycle, simply remove the cooking basket; the machine will automatically shut down. Place the cooking basket back into the Air Fryer drawer and the cooking cycle will automatically resume.

Use your Air Fryer to reheat leftovers by setting the temperature to 300 degrees F for up to 10 minutes.

For crunchy, bright cruciferous vegetables, you can place them in boiling water for 3 to 5 minutes before adding them to the Air Fryer basket. Lightly toss your veggies with olive oil or an herbed vinaigrette and place in the preheated Air Fryer basket. Always remember not to over-fill the cooking basket. It is also important to keep air-fried veggies warm until ready to serve.

As for French fries, baking this favorite food is much healthier cooking method than deep-frying. Here's the secret to perfect fries. Cut your potatoes into 1/4-inch lengthwise pieces; make sure that the pieces are of uniform size; now, soak them in cold water for 30 minutes (45 minutes for sweet potato fries). You can add the vinegar to the water as well. Your fries will turn out slightly crispier and vinegar can improve their flavor too. When ready to eat, drain and pat them dry with a kitchen towel. Choose oil with a high smoke point such as olive oil, canola oil or clarified duck fat; when you're making sweet potato fries, coconut oil is an excellent choice because it will give a unique flavor to your favorite fries. Try not to crowd the fries in the Air Fryer basket. Afterwards, place them on a cooling rack set over a baking sheet – it is a little trick to keep your fries crispy until ready to serve. Salt your fries while they are still hot. Needless to say, use the best ingredients you can find.

## 7 Mistakes to Avoid with Your Air Fryer

Here are seven common mistakes people make when using Air Fryers – and how to avoid them.

**You don't read instructions before beginning.** When using an electrical appliance, basic manufacturer's instructions should always be followed; this is extremely important for safety reasons. That way, you'll avoid common mistakes.

**You tend to overcrowd basket.** We have said it before, and we'll say it again: If you tend to overcrowd the cooking basket, you're not allowing the Air Fryer to do its job properly. Crispy and slightly browned veggies are much more appealing and tasty than ones that are mushy and pale because of overcrowding. Therefore, for better results, give your food some breathing room in the cooking basket. Work in a few batches, and if you're in a hurry, cook smaller pieces of food. Larger Air Fryers can make the cooking process a little easier; keep that in mind if you are considering buying a new kitchen appliance. Anyway, never fill the Air Fryer basket more than 80% capacity.

**You cook too small and lightweight items.** As we said before, an Air Fryer has a powerful fan on top of the unit. It is not suitable for foods such as egg roll wrappers and lightweight freeze-dried foods, so be careful.

**Your foods turn out dry and tasteless.** Foods can dry out quickly on high temperatures; they can also come out stuck together. If your veggies turn out limp and mushy, this is a timing issue. Therefore, you should modify the temperature and time for certain food. If you are not sure, simply go 30 degrees F below and cut the time by 20 to 30 percent. Then, check your food and increase the cooking time if necessary.

**You do not want to invest in some accessories.** Accessories such as baking pans and oven-safe dishes have to be able to fit inside the cooking basket. Another important rule – they shouldn't come into contact with the heating element.

**You're using wet coatings.** Do not worry, wet battered foods such as tempura can be adapted to the Air Fryer. Coat your food generously with a crisp coating like breadcrumbs, crushed crackers, crushed tortilla chips, or pork rinds. Try to apply a classic three-step breading procedure (flour, eggs, and breadcrumbs) to reduce splattering.

**You are afraid of mistakes.** Mistakes are natural; they are also a big part of how we learn. Give yourself enough time to learn and enjoy a new cooking method. Remember, there is a time to plant and a time to harvest. Recipes can't be rushed if you want a delicious, perfectly cooked food.

## Converting Traditional Recipes to the Air Fryer

Any ingredient that can be cooked in a microwave, conventional, convection, or toaster oven can be cooked in the Air Fryer. Simply put, air frying is just like baked and fried food in one. However, everything has its pros and cons so one of biggest disadvantages of Air Fryers is that they are smaller than standard ovens. Your favorite dinner, such as roasted meat with potatoes usually take 1 hour in the standard oven; it will take only 40 minutes in the Air Fryer. Add to this that instead of having to submerge ingredients in a lot of oil to make them flavorful and crispy, you will need a tablespoon or two of healthy vegetable oil.

Keep in mind that the heat in the Air Fryer is more intense than a conventional oven, so reduce the temperature by 25 to 50 degrees F. Slightly adjust the time by cooking your food for 20 to 30 percent less time. If you are not sure, simply start with less time and gradually adjust. Some authors recommend starting by cutting the time in half since the Air Fryer is much smaller than a conventional oven, so the heat is delivered inside the cooking basket more efficiently. What does it look like in practice?

If your recipe calls for roasting in the oven at 400 degrees F for 40 minutes, instead you should cook your food in the Air Fryer at 370 degrees F for about 30 minutes. Try using the cooking charts below to help determine the right cooking time for certain foods. Our chart features favorite Air Fryer foods, so that if you do not feel like reading recipes, then you can quickly check this list. Typically, most foods will cook at 360 to 380 degrees F; if you want ingredients more crispy, then cook them at 400 degrees F; if you want to slow cook your food, simply use lower temperatures. You can also try an online Air Fryer Calculator, which will easily convert oven guideline cooking temperatures and times to Air Fryer cooking times and temperatures. You can also find plenty of information about the Air Fryer frozen food times and temperatures. It includes favorite items like frozen chicken wings, shrimp, fries, mozzarella sticks, corn dog, fish sticks, hash browns, burritos, chicken tenders, pastries, tater tots, and so on.

Remember to check your foods for doneness. As with all cooking methods, it makes sense to open the lid and check the foods as they cook. Just remember to turn your food over halfway through the cooking time. As for small items like fries, you should test them every 5 to 10 minutes during cooking time. The same rule applies to packaged foods. And last but not least, it is incredibly important to choose the right size of the Air Fryer (the cooking baskets measure from 2 to 5.8 quarts). As you can see, using the Air Fryer isn't rocket science.

## The Benefits of Using an Air Fryer

**Health.** Is the air frying a healthy cooking method? Deep fried foods absorb fat, which significantly increases their calorie content. Furthermore, these foods are typically coated in breadcrumbs, flour, or eggs prior to frying. For instance, a medium-sized baked potato (approximately 100 grams) contains about 93 calories, 0 grams of fat and 0 milligrams of cholesterol. On the other hand, 100 grams of French fries contain 319 calories and 17 grams of fat; they also contain high amounts of trans-fats and sodium (approximately 234 milligrams).

In fact, you should not be afraid of fat, you should avoid a harmful fat in a deep fryer oil that contains free radicals. Vegetable oils to avoid include soybean oil, corn oil, cottonseed oil, sunflower oil, peanut oil, and rice bran oil. Oils with health benefits include olive oil, coconut oil, grapeseed oil, flaxseed oil, avocado oil, walnut oil, and sesame oil. Butter, tallow, and lard are excellent for frying because they have a high smoke point. Unfortunately, healthy and unrefined oils have a low smoke point and they become unhealthy under the heat in deep fryers. It is better to save them for salad dressings and cook your food with minimum oil.

Researches have hypothesized that eating too much "bad" oil can lead to increased inflammation in the body. What is worse, bad oils increase the amount of harmful LDL cholesterol in the bloodstream and speed up aging. Even small amounts of trans-fats can increase the risk of heart disease by 23%.

As for the Air Fryers, spritz non-stick oil all over ingredients in the cooking basket. You will end up with a perfect crunchy bite and moist interiors without submerging food in hot oil. As for the type of oil, connoisseurs recommend grapeseed, avocado, and light olive oil; they all have a high smoke point and neutral flavor. Sesame oil, with its rich and unique flavor, might be great for savory meals, but it is not a good choice for making a dessert. Avoid corn oil, palm oil, and soybean oil at all costs; these oils are partially hydrogenated, genetically modified and loaded with trans-fats. Margarine and fake butter alternatives should be avoided as well.

With this in mind, the Air Fryer will inspire you to cook healthy and well-balanced meals for your family.

**Fast cooking.** Cooking times in the Air Fryer are shorter in comparison with standard convection oven or convection toaster oven. Your Air Fryer heats up in a few minutes, then, hot air circulates quickly, cooking your food evenly on all sides. It can take about 50 minutes to roast chicken in a conventional oven; in an Air Fryer, it gets perfectly cooked, beautifully browned with crispy edges in 30 to 35 minutes. Many Air Fryer models come with dividers so that you can cook different dishes at the same time. The Air Fryer is a real winner for one-pot meals too. This is a space, cost, and frustration saving solution!

**Convenience**. The convenience and ease of use are one of the best features of your Air Fryer. With a user-friendly design, a simple touch operation and an "on/off" switch, an Air Fryer can be a great choice. In fact, cooking specifications are preprogrammed in advance and all you have to do is to push a button and go about your business. This intelligent machine will do the rest. If you often forget about food when it's cooking, an Air Fryer will give you peace of mind since it has a digital countdown timer and buzzer. In addition, the heat is maintained throughout the cooking time, eliminating the need to set cooking temperatures and watch over frying pans. On the other hand, you can stay in control of the cooking process since temperatures can be adjusted at any time and your device can be turned OFF at any time too.

Another convenience is that an Air Fryer won't smoke up your kitchen. Food baskets can easily be cleaned in a dishwasher. You can also use a sponge and a mild dishwashing soap. Besides being convenient, air fryers are safe to use.

**More flavor.** These fried foods do not taste like fat. These fried foods are really delicious! Extraordinary chips are only the beginning. Old-fashioned casseroles, spicy chilies, perfect mac and cheese, sophisticated appetizers, ooey-gooey bread puddings and delicious snacks turn out great in the Air Fryer.

All these advantages, make your Air Fryer a great choice when it comes to healthy dieting that does not compromise convenience and flavor.

# Air Fryer Cooking Guide

| CHICKEN | Temperature | Time (minutes) | | Temperature | Time (minutes) |
| --- | --- | --- | --- | --- | --- |
| Breasts, bone in | 370°F | 20-25 | Nuggets | 390°F | 6-10 |
| Chicken wings | 360°F | 15-20 | Whole chicken | 360°F | 70-75 |
| Game Hen | 390°F | 20-22 | Tenders | 360°F | 8-10 |
| Legs | 370°F | 20-22 | Thighs, boneless | 380°F | 18-20 |
| Legs, bone in | 380°F | 28-30 | Thighs, bone in | 380°F | 20-22 |

**BEEF**

| | Temperature | Time (minutes) | | Temperature | Time (minutes) |
| --- | --- | --- | --- | --- | --- |
| Burger | 370°F | 16-20 | Meatballs (big) | 380°F | 10-12 |
| Filet mignon | 400°F | 18 | Ribeye | 400°F | 10-15 |
| Flank steak | 400°F | 12-15 | Round roast | 390°F | 45-55 |
| London broil | 400°F | 20-28 | Sirloin steaks | 400°F | 9-15 |
| Meatballs (1-inch) | 380°F | 7-10 | | | |

**PORK and LAMB**

| | Temperature | Time (minutes) | | Temperature | Time (minutes) |
| --- | --- | --- | --- | --- | --- |
| Bacon | 400°F | 5-7 | Rack of lamb | 380°F | 22 |
| Bacon (thick cut) | 400°F | 6-10 | Sausages | 380°F | 12-15 |
| Lamb loin chops | 400°F | 6-10 | Spare ribs | 400°F | 18-25 |
| Loin | 360°F | 50-55 | Tenderloin | 400°F | 5-8 |
| Pork chops | 400°F | 12-15 | | | |

**FISH**

| | Temperature | Time (minutes) | | Temperature | Time (minutes) |
| --- | --- | --- | --- | --- | --- |
| Calamari | 400°F | 4-5 | Swordfish steak | 400°F | 10-12 |
| Fish sticks | 390°F | 6-10 | Tuna steak | 400°F | 8-10 |
| Fish fillet | 400°F | 10-12 | Scallops | 400°F | 5-7 |
| Salmon (fillet) | 380°F | 12 | Shrimp | 400°F | 5-6 |
| Shellfish | 400°F | 12-15 | | | |

**VEGETABLES**

| | Temperature | Time (minutes) | | Temperature | Time (minutes) |
| --- | --- | --- | --- | --- | --- |
| Asparagus | 400°F | 5-7 | Mushrooms | 400°F | 5 |
| Beets | 400°F | 40 | Onions | 400°F | 8-10 |
| Broccoli | 400°F | 6 | Parsnip | 380°F | 15 |
| Brussels Sprouts | 380°F | 15 | Peppers | 400°F | 15 |
| Carrots | 380°F | 13-15 | Potatoes | 400°F | 12 |
| Cauliflower | 400°F | 12-15 | Potatoes (baby) | 400°F | 15 |
| Corn on the cob | 390°F | 6-10 | Squash | 400°F | 12-15 |
| Eggplant | 400°F | 15 | Sweet potato | 380°F | 35 |
| Fennel | 370°F | 15 | Tomato (cherry) | 380°F | 20-22 |
| Green beans | 400°F | 5-7 | Tomato | 350°F | 10 |
| Kale | 250°F | 12 | Zucchini | 400°F | 10 |

**FROZEN FOOD**

| | Temperature | Time (minutes) | | Temperature | Time (minutes) |
| --- | --- | --- | --- | --- | --- |
| Breaded shrimp | 400°F | 10-12 | Mozzarella stick | 400°F | 8-10 |
| Fish fillets | 400°F | 14-20 | Onion rings | 400°F | 8 |
| Fish sticks | 400°F | 10-12 | Pot stickers | 400°F | 8-10 |
| French fries (thin) | 400°F | 15-20 | | | |

# POULTRY

## Peanut Chicken and Pepper Wraps

*(Ready in about 25 minutes | Servings 4)*
**Per serving:** 529 Calories; 25.5g Fat; 31.5g Carbs; 40.1g Protein; 6.8g Sugars

### Ingredients

1 ½ pounds chicken breast, boneless and skinless
1/4 cup peanut butter
1 tablespoon sesame oil
1 tablespoon soy sauce
2 teaspoons rice vinegar
1 teaspoon fresh ginger, peeled and grated
1 teaspoon fresh garlic, minced
1 teaspoon brown sugar
2 tablespoons lemon juice, freshly squeezed
4 tortillas
1 bell pepper, julienned

### Directions

Start by preheating your Air Fryer to 380 degrees F.

Cook the chicken breasts in the preheated Air Fryer approximately 6 minutes. Turn them over and cook an additional 6 minutes.

Meanwhile, make the sauce by mixing the peanut butter, sesame oil, soy sauce, vinegar, ginger, garlic, sugar, and lemon juice.

Slice the chicken crosswise across the grain into 1/4-inch strips. Toss the chicken into the sauce.

Decrease temperature to 390 degrees F. Spoon the chicken and sauce onto each tortilla; add bell peppers and wrap them tightly.

Drizzle with a nonstick cooking spray and bake about 7 minutes. Serve warm.

## Sausage, Ham and Hash Brown Bake

*(Ready in about 45 minutes | Servings 4)*
**Per serving:** 509 Calories; 20.1g Fat; 40g Carbs; 41.2g Protein; 3.9g Sugars

### Ingredients

1/2 pound chicken sausages, smoked
1/2 pound ham, sliced
6 ounces hash browns, frozen and shredded
2 garlic cloves, minced
8 ounces spinach
1/2 cup Ricotta cheese
1/2 cup Asiago cheese, grated
4 eggs
1/2 cup yogurt
1/2 cup milk
Salt and ground black pepper, to taste
1 teaspoon smoked paprika

### Directions

Start by preheating your Air Fryer to 380 degrees F. Cook the sausages and ham for 10 minutes; set aside.

Meanwhile, in a preheated saucepan, cook the hash browns and garlic for 4 minutes, stirring frequently; remove from the heat, add the spinach and cover with the lid.

Allow the spinach to wilt completely. Transfer the sautéed mixture to a baking pan. Add the reserved sausage and ham.

In a mixing dish, thoroughly combine the cheese, eggs, yogurt, milk, salt, pepper, and paprika. Pour the cheese mixture over the hash browns in the pan.

Place the baking pan in the cooking basket and cook approximately 30 minutes or until everything is thoroughly cooked. Bon appétit!

# The Best Chicken Burgers Ever

*(Ready in about 20 minutes | Servings 4)*

**Per serving:** 507 Calories; 26.5g Fat; 37.6g Carbs; 30g Protein; 12.8g Sugars

*Ingredients*

1 tablespoon olive oil

1 onion, peeled and finely chopped

2 garlic cloves, minced

Sea salt and ground black pepper, to taste

1/2 teaspoon paprika

1/2 teaspoon ground cumin

1 pound chicken breast, ground

4 soft rolls

4 tablespoons ketchup

4 tablespoons mayonnaise

2 teaspoons Dijon mustard

4 tablespoons green onions, chopped

4 pickles, sliced

*Directions*

Heat the olive oil in a skillet over high flame. Then, sauté the onion until golden and translucent, about 4 minutes.

Add the garlic and cook an additional 30 seconds or until it is aromatic. Season with salt, pepper, paprika, and cumin; reserve.

Add the chicken and cook for 2 to 3 minutes, stirring and crumbling with a fork. Add the onion mixture and mix to combine well.

Shape the mixture into patties and transfer them to the cooking basket. Cook in the preheated Air Fryer at 360 degrees F for 6 minutes. Turn them over and cook an additional 5 minutes. Work in batches.

Smear the base of the roll with ketchup, mayo, and mustard. Top with the chicken, green onions, and pickles. Enjoy!

# Marinated Chicken Drumettes with Asparagus

*(Ready in about 30 minutes + marinating time | Servings 6)*

**Per serving:** 356 Calories; 22.1g Fat; 7.8g Carbs; 31.4g Protein; 4.1g Sugars

*Ingredients*

6 chicken drumettes

1 ½ pounds asparagus, ends trimmed

Marinade:

3 tablespoons canola oil

3 tablespoons soy sauce

3 tablespoons lime juice

3 heaping tablespoons shallots, minced

1 heaping teaspoon fresh garlic, minced

1 (1-inch) piece fresh ginger, peeled and minced

1 teaspoon Creole seasoning

Coarse sea salt and ground black pepper, to taste

*Directions*

In a ceramic bowl, mix all ingredients for the marinade. Add the chicken drumettes and let them marinate at least 5 hours in the refrigerator. Now, drain the chicken drumettes and discard the marinade.

Cook in the preheated Air Fryer at 370 degrees F for 11 minutes. Turn the chicken drumettes over and cook for a further 11 minutes.

While the chicken drumettes are cooking, add the reserved marinade to the preheated skillet. Add the asparagus and cook for approximately 5 minutes or until cooked through. Serve with the air-fried chicken and enjoy!

# Easy Chicken Sliders

*(Ready in about 30 minutes | Servings 3)*

**Per serving:** 479 Calories; 17.9g Fat; 43g Carbs; 34.4g Protein; 1.3g Sugars

*Ingredients*

1/2 cup all-purpose flour

1 teaspoon garlic salt

1/2 teaspoon black pepper, preferably freshly ground

1 teaspoon celery seeds

1/2 teaspoon mustard seeds

1/2 teaspoon dried basil

1 egg

2 chicken breasts, cut in thirds

6 small-sized dinner rolls

*Directions*

In mixing bowl, thoroughly combine the flour and seasonings.

In a separate shallow bowl, beat the egg until frothy.

Dredge the chicken through the flour mixture, then into egg; afterwards, roll them over the flour mixture again.

Spritz the chicken pieces with a cooking spray on all sides. Transfer them to the cooking basket.

Cook in the preheated Air Fryer at 380 degrees F for 15 minutes; turn them over and cook an additional 10 to 12 minutes.

Test for doneness and adjust the seasonings. Serve immediately on dinner rolls.

# Turkey and Sausage Meatloaf with Herbs

*(Ready in about 45 minutes | Servings 4)*

**Per serving:** 431 Calories; 22.3g Fat; 32.6g Carbs; 25.9g Protein; 18.5g Sugars

*Ingredients*

1/2 cup milk

4 bread slices, crustless

1 tablespoon olive oil

1 onion, finely chopped

1 garlic clove, minced

1/2 pound ground turkey

1/2 pound ground breakfast sausage

1 duck egg, whisked

1 teaspoon rosemary

1 teaspoon basil

1 teaspoon thyme

1 teaspoon cayenne pepper

Kosher salt and ground black pepper, to taste

1/2 cup ketchup

2 tablespoons molasses

1 tablespoon brown mustard

*Directions*

In a shallow bowl, pour the milk over the bread and let it soak in for 5 to 6 minutes.

Heat 1 tablespoon of oil over medium-high heat in a nonstick pan. Sauté the onions and garlic until tender and fragrant, about 2 minutes.

Add the turkey, sausage, egg, rosemary, basil, thyme, cayenne pepper, salt, and ground black pepper. Stir in the milk-soaked bread. Mix until everything is well incorporated.

Shape the mixture into a loaf and transfer it to a pan that is lightly greased with an olive oil mister. Next, lower the pan onto the cooking basket.

In a mixing bowl, whisk the ketchup with molasses and mustard. Spread this mixture over the top of your meatloaf.

Cook approximately 27 minutes or until the meatloaf is no longer pink in the middle. Allow it to sit 10 minutes before slicing and serving. Bon appétit!

# Turkey Wings with Butter Roasted Potatoes

*(Ready in about 55 minutes | Servings 4)*

**Per serving:** 567 Calories; 14.3g Fat; 65.7g Carbs; 46.1g Protein; 2.9g Sugars

*Ingredients*
4 large-sized potatoes, peeled and cut into 1-inch chunks
1 tablespoon butter, melted
1 teaspoon rosemary
1 teaspoon garlic salt
1/2 teaspoon ground black pepper
1 ½ pounds turkey wings
2 tablespoons olive oil
2 garlic cloves, minced
1 tablespoon Dijon mustard
1/2 teaspoon cayenne pepper

*Directions*
Add the potatoes, butter, rosemary, salt, and pepper to the cooking basket.
Cook at 400 degrees F for 12 minutes. Reserve the potatoes, keeping them warm.
Now, place the turkey wings in the cooking basket that is previously cleaned and greased with olive oil. Add the garlic, mustard, and cayenne pepper.
Cook in the preheated Air Fryer at 350 degrees f for 25 minutes. Turn them over and cook an additional 15 minutes.
Test for doneness with a meat thermometer. Serve with warm potatoes.

# Smoked Duck with Rosemary-Infused Gravy

*(Ready in about 30 minutes | Servings 4)*

**Per serving:** 485 Calories; 19.7g Fat; 24.1g Carbs; 51.3g Protein; 15.6g Sugars

*Ingredients*
1 ½ pounds smoked duck breasts, boneless
1 tablespoon yellow mustard
2 tablespoons ketchup
1 teaspoon agave syrup
12 pearl onions peeled
1 tablespoon flour
5 ounces chicken broth
1 teaspoon rosemary, finely chopped

*Directions*
Cook the smoked duck breasts in the preheated Air Fryer at 365 degrees F for 15 minutes.
Smear the mustard, ketchup, and agave syrup on the duck breast. Top with pearl onions. Cook for a further 7 minutes or until the skin of the duck breast looks crispy and golden brown.
Slice the duck breasts and reserve. Drain off the duck fat from the pan.
Then, add the reserved 1 tablespoon of duck fat to the pan and warm it over medium heat; add flour and cook until your roux is dark brown.
Add the chicken broth and rosemary to the pan. Reduce the heat to low and cook until the gravy has thickened slightly. Spoon the warm gravy over the reserved duck breasts. Enjoy!

# Farmhouse Roast Turkey

*(Ready in about 50 minutes | Servings 6)*

**Per serving:** 316 Calories; 24.2g Fat; 2.5g Carbs; 20.4g Protein; 1.1g Sugars

*Ingredients*
2 pounds turkey
1 tablespoon fresh rosemary, chopped
1 teaspoon sea salt
1/2 teaspoon ground black pepper
1 onion, chopped
1 celery stalk, chopped

*Directions*

Start by preheating your Air Fryer to 360 degrees F. Spritz the sides and bottom of the cooking basket with a nonstick cooking spray.

Place the turkey in the cooking basket. Add the rosemary, salt, and black pepper. Cook for 30 minutes in the preheated Air Fryer.

Add the onion and celery and cook an additional 15 minutes. Bon appétit!

## Chicken with Golden Roasted Cauliflower

*(Ready in about 30 minutes | Servings 4)*
**Per serving:** 388 Calories; 18.9g Fat; 5.6g Carbs; 47.3g Protein; 1.3g Sugars

*Ingredients*
2 pounds chicken legs
2 tablespoons olive oil
1 teaspoon sea salt
1/2 teaspoon ground black pepper
1 teaspoon smoked paprika
1 teaspoon dried marjoram
1 (1-pound) head cauliflower, broken into small florets
2 garlic cloves, minced
1/3 cup Pecorino Romano cheese, freshly grated
1/2 teaspoon dried thyme
Salt, to taste

*Directions*
Toss the chicken legs with the olive oil, salt, black pepper, paprika, and marjoram.

Cook in the preheated Air Fryer at 380 degrees F for 11 minutes. Flip the chicken legs and cook for a further 5 minutes.

Toss the cauliflower florets with garlic, cheese, thyme, and salt.

Increase the temperature to 400 degrees F; add the cauliflower florets and cook for 12 more minutes. Serve warm.

## Adobo Seasoned Chicken with Veggies

*(Ready in about 1 hour 30 minutes | Servings 4)*
**Per serving:** 427 Calories; 15.3g Fat; 18.5g Carbs; 52.3g Protein; 9.4g Sugars

*Ingredients*
2 pounds chicken wings, rinsed and patted dry
1 teaspoon coarse sea salt
1/4 teaspoon ground black pepper
1/2 teaspoon red pepper flakes, crushed
1 teaspoon ground cumin
1 teaspoon paprika
1 teaspoon granulated onion
1 teaspoon ground turmeric
2 tablespoons tomato powder
1 tablespoon dry Madeira wine
2 stalks celery, diced
2 cloves garlic, peeled but not chopped
1 large Spanish onion, diced
2 bell peppers, seeded and sliced
4 carrots, trimmed and halved
2 tablespoons olive oil

*Directions*
Toss all ingredients in a large bowl. Cover and let it sit for 1 hour in your refrigerator.

Add the chicken wings to a baking pan.

Roast the chicken wings in the preheated Air Fryer at 380 degrees F for 7 minutes.

Add the vegetables and cook an additional 15 minutes, shaking the basket once or twice. Serve warm.

# Spice Lime Chicken Tenders

*(Ready in about 20 minutes | Servings 6)*

**Per serving:** 422 Calories; 29.2g Fat; 6.1g Carbs; 32.9g Protein; 2.4g Sugars

### Ingredients

1 lime

2 pounds chicken tenderloins cut up

1 cup cornflakes, crushed

1/2 cup Parmesan cheese, grated

1 tablespoon olive oil

Sea salt and ground black pepper, to taste

1 teaspoon cayenne pepper

1/3 teaspoon ground cumin

1 teaspoon chili powder

1 egg

### Directions

Squeeze the lime juice all over the chicken.

Spritz the cooking basket with a nonstick cooking spray.

In a mixing bowl, thoroughly combine the cornflakes, Parmesan, olive oil, salt, black pepper, cayenne pepper, cumin, and chili powder.

In another shallow bowl, whisk the egg until well beaten. Dip the chicken tenders in the egg, then in cornflakes mixture.

Transfer the breaded chicken to the prepared cooking basket. Cook in the preheated Air Fryer at 380 degrees F for 12 minutes. Turn them over halfway through the cooking time. Work in batches. Serve immediately.

# Quick and Easy Chicken Mole

*(Ready in about 35 minutes | Servings 4)*

**Per serving:** 453 Calories; 17.5g Fat; 25.1g Carbs; 47.5g Protein; 12.9g Sugars

### Ingredients

8 chicken thighs, skinless, bone-in

1 tablespoon peanut oil

Sea salt and ground black pepper, to taste

Mole sauce:

1 tablespoon peanut oil

1 onion, chopped

1 ounce dried negro chiles, stemmed, seeded, and chopped

2 garlic cloves, peeled and halved

2 large-sized fresh tomatoes, pureed

2 tablespoons raisins

1 ½ ounces bittersweet chocolate, chopped

1 teaspoon dried Mexican oregano

1/2 teaspoon ground cumin

1 teaspoon coriander seeds

A pinch of ground cloves

4 strips orange peel

1/4 cup almonds, sliced and toasted

### Directions

Start by preheating your Air Fryer to 380 degrees F. Toss the chicken thighs with the peanut oil, salt, and black pepper.

Cook in the preheated Air Fryer for 12 minutes; flip them and cook an additional 10 minutes; reserve.

To make the sauce, heat 1 tablespoon of peanut oil in a saucepan over medium-high heat. Now, sauté the onion, chiles and garlic until fragrant or about 2 minutes.

Next, stir in the tomatoes, raisins, chocolate, oregano, cumin, coriander seeds, and cloves. Let it simmer until the sauce has slightly thickened.

Add the reserved chicken to the baking pan; add the sauce and cook in the preheated Air Fryer at 360 degrees F for 10 minutes or until thoroughly warmed.

Serve garnished with orange peel and sliced almonds. Enjoy!

# Chicken Sausage Frittata with Cheese

*(Ready in about 15 minutes | Servings 2)*
**Per serving:** 475 Calories; 34.2g Fat; 5.3g Carbs; 36.2g Protein; 2.6g Sugars

*Ingredients*
1 tablespoon olive oil
2 chicken sausages, sliced
4 eggs
1 garlic clove, minced
1/2 yellow onion, chopped
Sea salt and ground black pepper, to taste
4 tablespoons Monterey-Jack cheese
1 tablespoon fresh parsley leaves, chopped

*Directions*
Grease the sides and bottom of a baking pan with olive oil.
Add the sausages and cook in the preheated Air Fryer at 360 degrees F for 4 to 5 minutes.
In a mixing dish, whisk the eggs with garlic and onion. Season with salt and black pepper.
Pour the mixture over sausages. Top with cheese. Cook in the preheated Air Fryer at 360 degrees F for another 6 minutes.
Serve immediately with fresh parsley leaves. Bon appétit!

# Traditional Chicken Teriyaki

*(Ready in about 50 minutes | Servings 4)*
**Per serving:** 362 Calories; 21.1g Fat; 4.4g Carbs; 36.6g Protein; 2.4g Sugars

*Ingredients*
1 ½ pounds chicken breast, halved
1 tablespoon lemon juice
2 tablespoons Mirin
1/4 cup milk
2 tablespoons soy sauce

1 tablespoon olive oil
1 teaspoon ginger, peeled and grated
2 garlic cloves, minced
1/2 teaspoon salt
1/2 teaspoon ground black pepper
1 teaspoon cornstarch

*Directions*
In a large ceramic dish, place the chicken, lemon juice, Mirin, milk, soy sauce, olive oil, ginger, and garlic. Let it marinate for 30 minutes in your refrigerator.
Spritz the sides and bottom of the cooking basket with a nonstick cooking spray. Arrange the chicken in the cooking basket and cook at 370 degrees F for 10 minutes.
Turn over the chicken, baste with the reserved marinade and cook for 4 minutes longer. Taste for doneness, season with salt and pepper, and reserve.
Mix the cornstarch with 1 tablespoon of water. Add the marinade to the preheated skillet over medium heat; cook for 3 to 4 minutes. Now, stir in the cornstarch slurry and cook until the sauce thickens.
Spoon the sauce over the reserved chicken and serve immediately.

# Loaded Chicken Burgers

*(Ready in about 30 minutes | Servings 5)*
**Per serving:** 476 Calories; 25.9g Fat; 29.9g Carbs; 31.7g Protein; 2.5g Sugars

*Ingredients*
2 tablespoons olive oil
1 onion, finely chopped
2 green garlic, chopped
6 ounces mushrooms, chopped
1 ½ pounds ground chicken
1/3 cup parmesan cheese

1/4 cup pork rinds, crushed

1 tablespoon fish sauce

1 tablespoon tamari sauce

1 teaspoon Dijon mustard

5 soft hamburger buns

5 lettuce leaves

### Directions

Heat a nonstick skillet over medium-high heat; add olive oil. Once hot, sauté the onion until tender and translucent, about 3 minutes.

Add the garlic and mushrooms and cook an additional 2 minutes, stirring frequently.

Add the ground chicken, cheese, pork rind, fish sauce, and tamari sauce; mix until everything is well incorporated.

Form the mixture into 5 patties. Transfer the patties to the lightly greased cooking basket.

Cook in the preheated Air Fryer at 370 degrees F for 8 minutes; then, flip them over and cook for 8 minutes on the other side.

Serve on burger buns, garnished with mustard and lettuce. Bon appétit!

## Chicken and Brown Rice Bake

*(Ready in about 50 minutes | Servings 3)*

**Per serving:** 508 Calories; 18.3g Fat; 61g Carbs; 24.5g Protein; 7.2g Sugars

### Ingredients

1 cup brown rice

2 cups vegetable broth

1/2 cup water

1 tablespoon butter, melted

1 onion, chopped

2 garlic cloves, minced

Kosher salt and ground black pepper, to taste

1 teaspoon cayenne pepper

3 chicken fillets

1 cup tomato puree

1 tablespoon fresh chives, chopped

### Directions

Heat the brown rice, vegetable broth and water in a pot over high heat. Bring it to a boil; turn the stove down to simmer and cook for 35 minutes. Grease a baking pan with butter.

Spoon the prepared rice mixture into the baking pan. Add the onion, garlic, salt, black pepper, cayenne pepper, and chicken. Spoon the tomato puree over the chicken.

Cook in the preheated Air Fryer at 380 degrees F for 12 minutes. Serve garnished with fresh chives. Enjoy!

## Sticky Exotic Chicken Drumettes

*(Ready in about 25 minutes | Servings 4)*

**Per serving:** 317 Calories; 12.5g Fat; 11.5g Carbs; 38.4g Protein; 10.1g Sugars

### Ingredients

2 tablespoons peanut oil

2 tablespoons honey

1 tablespoon tamari sauce

1 tablespoon yellow mustard

1 clove garlic, peeled and minced

2 tablespoons fresh orange juice

1/2 teaspoon sambal oelek

1 ½ pounds chicken drumettes, bone-in

Salt and ground white pepper, to taste

1/4 cup chicken broth

1/2 cup raw onion rings, for garnish

### Directions

Start by preheating your Air Fryer to 380 degrees F.

Line the cooking basket with parchment paper. Lightly grease the parchment paper with 1 tablespoon of peanut oil.

In a mixing bowl, thoroughly combine the remaining 1 tablespoon of oil, honey, tamari sauce, mustard, garlic, orange juice, and sambal oelek. Whisk to combine well.

Arrange the chicken drumettes in the prepared cooking basket. Season with salt and white pepper.

Spread 1/2 of the honey mixture evenly all over each breast. Pour in the chicken broth. Cook for 12 minutes.

Turn them over, add the remaining 1/2 of the honey mixture, and cook an additional 10 minutes.

Garnish with onion rings and serve immediately.

## Spanish Chicken with Golden Potatoes

*(Ready in about 25 minutes | Servings 4)*
**Per serving:** 382 Calories; 17.9g Fat; 26.1g Carbs; 26.7g Protein; 1.6g Sugars

### Ingredients

2 tablespoons butter, melted
4 chicken drumsticks, bone-in
1 pound Yukon Gold potatoes, peeled and diced
1 lemon, 1/2 juiced, 1/2 cut into wedges
1 teaspoon fresh garlic, minced
1 teaspoon dried rosemary, crushed
1 teaspoon dried thyme, crushed
1 teaspoon cayenne pepper
1/3 teaspoon freshly ground black pepper
Kosher salt, to taste
2 tablespoons sherry

### Directions

Start by preheating your Air Fryer to 370 degrees F. Then, grease a baking pan with the melted butter. Arrange the chicken drumsticks in the baking pan.

Bake in the preheated Air Fryer for 8 minutes. Add the diced potatoes. Drizzle chicken and potatoes with lemon juice. Sprinkle with garlic, rosemary, thyme, cayenne pepper, black pepper, and salt.

Turn the temperature to 400 degrees F and cook for a further 12 minutes. Make sure to shake the basket once or twice.

Remove from the Air Fryer basket and sprinkle sherry on top. Serve with the lemon wedges. Enjoy!

## Turkey Breakfast Frittata

*(Ready in about 50 minutes | Servings 4)*
**Per serving:** 327 Calories; 13.4g Fat; 3.5g Carbs; 45.4g Protein; 2.3g Sugars

### Ingredients

1 tablespoon olive oil
1 pound turkey breasts, slices
6 large-sized eggs
3 tablespoons Greek yogurt
3 tablespoons Cottage cheese, crumbled
1/4 teaspoon ground black pepper
1/4 teaspoon red pepper flakes, crushed
Himalayan salt, to taste
1 red bell pepper, seeded and sliced
1 green bell pepper, seeded and sliced

### Directions

Grease the cooking basket with olive oil. Add the turkey and cook in the preheated Air Fryer at 350 degrees F for 30 minutes, flipping them over halfway through. Cut into bite-sized strips and reserve.

Now, beat the eggs with Greek yogurt, cheese, black pepper, red pepper, and salt. Add the bell peppers to a baking pan that is previously lightly greased with a cooking spray.

Add the turkey strips; pour the egg mixture over all ingredients.

Bake in the preheated Air Fryer at 360 degrees F for 15 minutes. Serve right away!

# Nana's Turkey Chili

*(Ready in about 1 hour | Servings 4)*

**Per serving:** 327 Calories; 13.4g Fat; 3.5g Carbs; 45.4g Protein; 2.3g Sugars

*Ingredients*

1/2 medium-sized leek, chopped

1/2 red onion, chopped

2 garlic cloves, minced

1 jalapeno pepper, seeded and minced

1 bell pepper, seeded and chopped

2 tablespoons olive oil

1 pound ground turkey, 85% lean 15% fat

2 cups tomato puree

2 cups chicken stock

1/2 teaspoon black peppercorns

Salt, to taste

1 teaspoon chili powder

1 teaspoon mustard seeds

1 teaspoon ground cumin

1 (12-ounce) can kidney beans, rinsed and drained

*Directions*

Start by preheating your Air Fryer to 365 degrees F.

Place the leeks, onion, garlic and peppers in a baking pan; drizzle olive oil evenly over the top. Cook for 4 to 6 minutes.

Add the ground turkey. Cook for 6 minutes more or until the meat is no longer pink.

Now, add the tomato puree, 1 cup of chicken stock, black peppercorns, salt, chili powder, mustard seeds, and cumin to the baking pan.

Cook for 24 minutes, stirring every 7 to 10 minutes.

Stir in the canned beans and the remaining 1 cup of stock; let it cook for a further 9 minutes; make sure to stir halfway through. Bon appétit!

# Delicious Turkey Sandwiches

*(Ready in about 45 minutes | Servings 4)*

**Per serving:** 427 Calories; 18g Fat; 33.5g Carbs; 32.8g Protein; 6.1g Sugars

*Ingredients*

1 pound turkey tenderloins

1 tablespoon Dijon-style mustard

1 tablespoon olive oil

Sea salt and ground black pepper, to taste

1 teaspoon Italian seasoning mix

1/4 cup all-purpose flour

1 cup turkey stock

8 slices sourdough, toasted

4 tablespoons tomato ketchup

4 tablespoons mayonnaise

4 pickles, sliced

*Directions*

Rub the turkey tenderloins with the mustard and olive oil. Season with salt, black pepper, and Italian seasoning mix.

Cook the turkey tenderloins at 350 degrees F for 30 minutes, flipping them over halfway through. Let them rest for 5 to 7 minutes before slicing.

For the gravy, in a saucepan, place the drippings from the roasted turkey. Add 1/8 cup of flour and 1/2 cup of turkey stock; whisk until it makes a smooth paste.

Once it gets a golden brown color, add the rest of the stock and flour. Season with salt to taste. Let it simmer over medium heat, stirring constantly for 6 to 7 minutes.

Assemble the sandwiches with the turkey, gravy, tomato ketchup, mayonnaise, and pickles. Serve and enjoy!

# Traditional Chicken Tetrazzini

*(Ready in about 55 minutes | Servings 4)*

**Per serving:** 427 Calories; 18g Fat; 33.5g Carbs; 32.8g Protein; 6.1g Sugars

*Ingredients*

10 ounces noodles, cooked
2 tablespoons olive oil
1 pound chicken breast
Sea salt and pepper, to taste
1 onion, sliced
2 garlic cloves, minced
1 can cream of chicken soup
1 can cream of mushroom soup
1 cup sour cream
1/2 cup mozzarella cheese, shredded

*Directions*

Bring a large pot of lightly salted water to a boil. Cook your noodles for 10 minutes or until al dente; drain and reserve, keeping warm.

Preheat your Air Fryer to 370 degrees F. Brush the cooking basket with 1 teaspoon of olive oil. Sprinkle the chicken breasts with salt and pepper. Cook for 25 minutes or until the chicken breasts are slightly browned.

Preheat your Air Fryer to 370 degrees F. Lightly grease the bottom and sides of the baking pan with the remaining 1 tablespoon of olive oil.

Add the onion, garlic, chicken soup, mushroom soup, and sour cream. Add the reserved noodles and the chicken.

Cook for 12 minutes in the preheated Air Fryer. Top with mozzarella and cook an additional 6 minutes until it is bubbling. Serve warm.

# Chicken Egg Rolls with Hot Dipping Sauce

*(Ready in about 35 minutes | Servings 5)*

**Per serving:** 350 Calories; 19.7g Fat; 20.6g Carbs; 21.2g Protein; 8.1g Sugars

*Ingredients*

2 teaspoons olive oil
1 pound ground chicken
Salt and ground pepper, to taste
2 scallions, sliced thinly
2 cloves garlic, finely chopped
2 cups Napa cabbage, shredded
2 tablespoons soy sauce
1 teaspoon Dijon mustard
10 egg roll wrappers
Dipping Sauce:
1/3 cup lite soy sauce
1/3 cup Champagne vinegar
2 tablespoons molasses
1 tablespoon sesame oil
1/2 teaspoon chili powder

*Directions*

In a cast-iron skillet, heat the oil until sizzling; now, add the ground chicken and cook for 3 to 4 minutes, crumbling with a fork. Season with salt and pepper.

Stir in the scallions, garlic, and cabbage. Continue to sauté for 4 minutes more. Remove from the heat; add the soy sauce and mustard and stir again.

Fill the egg roll wrappers, using 1 to 2 tablespoons of filling. Place the filling in the center of the wrapper. Roll the corner over the filling and brush it with water.

Fold in the sides of the wrapper and continue rolling until it is closed. Press to seal and brush it with water.

Cook in the preheated Air Fryer at 375 degrees F for 13 to 16 minutes, turning over halfway through. Work in batches.

In the meantime, combine all of the sauce ingredients in a mixing bowl. Serve immediately with the warm egg rolls.

# Easy Thanksgiving Crunchwrap

*(Ready in about 1 hour 15 minutes | Servings 4)*
**Per serving:** 706 Calories; 59.5g Fat; 14.9g Carbs; 27.4g Protein; 4.4g Sugars

*Ingredients*

2 tablespoons sesame oil

1 pound turkey breasts

1 tablespoon taco seasoning

2 onions, sliced

2 bell peppers, sliced

1 habanero pepper, sliced

8 corn tortillas, approx. 7-8-inch diameter

1/2 cup queso quesadilla

1 cup Manchego cheese, grated

1 ½ cups tortilla chips

1/2 cup mayonnaise

2 tablespoons lemon juice

1 teaspoon yellow mustard

1 1/2 cup pickled jalapenos, chopped

1/4 teaspoon dried dill weed

1/2 teaspoon Mexican oregano

*Directions*

Start by preheating your Air Fryer to 350 degrees F. Drizzle 1 tablespoon of sesame oil all over the turkey breasts and cook for 30 minutes, flipping them over halfway through.

Let them rest for 7 minutes; then, slice the turkey breast into strips, add the taco seasoning, and reserve.

Place the onions and peppers in the cooking basket. Cook in the preheated Air Fryer at 400 degrees F for 13 minutes; reserve.

Spritz the base of a baking pan with cooking oil. Divide the roasted turkey, pepper mixture and cheese between the tortillas. Top with tortilla chips.

Fold over your tortillas, then, arrange them in the baking pan. Drizzle the remaining 1 tablespoon of sesame oil over each tortilla. Bake at 185 degrees F for 24 minutes.

Meanwhile, make the sauce by mixing the mayonnaise with lemon juice, mustard, jalapeno, dill, and oregano. Serve with the warm tortillas. Enjoy!

# Double Cheese and Chicken Crescent Bake

*(Ready in about 20 minutes | Servings 4)*
**Per serving:** 518 Calories; 25.4g Fat; 38.3g Carbs; 32.7g Protein; 8.6g Sugars

*Ingredients*

8 ounces regular-sized crescent rolls

1 ½ cups cooked turkey, shredded

1/4 cup prepared warm gravy

1 teaspoon garlic powder

1/4 teaspoon cayenne pepper

Salt and black pepper, to taste

1/2 cup cream of mushroom soup with herbs

1 can milk

1/2 teaspoon freshly ground black pepper

1 cup Colby cheese, shredded

1/4 cup Parmesan cheese grated

2 tablespoons fresh cilantro leaves, roughly chopped

*Directions*

Start by preheating your Air Fryer to 350 degrees F. Now, spritz the sides and bottom of a baking pan with a nonstick cooking spray.

Roll out the crescent rolls. Top with the turkey and gravy. Sprinkle with the garlic powder, cayenne pepper, salt, and black pepper.

Roll up and arrange them in the prepared baking pan. Mix the soup, milk and 1/2 teaspoon of black pepper to make the sauce. Pour the sauce around the crescents. Top with the cheese.

Bake for 12 minutes or until the top is golden brown. Serve garnished with fresh cilantro leaves. Bon appétit!

# Authentic Chicken-Fajitas with Salsa

*(Ready in about 30 minutes | Servings 4)*

**Per serving:** 433 Calories; 14.5g Fat; 44.9g Carbs; 30.2g Protein; 6.6g Sugars

*Ingredients*

1 pound chicken tenderloins, chopped

Sea salt and ground black pepper, to your liking

1 teaspoon shallot powder

1 teaspoon fajita seasoning

2 bell peppers, seeded and diced

4 flour tortillas

Salsa

1 ancho chili pepper, seeded and finely chopped

2 ripe tomatoes, crushed

1 bunch fresh coriander, roughly chopped

1 lime

2 tablespoons extra-virgin olive oil

**Directions**

Toss the chicken with salt, pepper, shallot powder, and fajita seasoning mix.

Roast in the preheated Air Fryer at 390 degrees F for 9 minutes. Add the bell peppers and roast an additional 8 minutes.

For the salsa, mix the chilli, tomatoes and coriander. Squeeze over the juice of 1 lime; add olive oil and stir to combine well.

Warm the tortillas in your Air Fryer at 200 degrees F for 10 minutes.

Serve the chicken fajitas with tortilla and salsa. Enjoy!

# Pizza Spaghetti Casserole

*(Ready in about 30 minutes | Servings 4)*

**Per serving:** 472 Calories; 23.1g Fat; 28.6g Carbs; 38.2g Protein; 7.6g Sugars

*Ingredients*

8 ounces spaghetti

1 pound smoked chicken sausage, sliced

2 tomatoes, pureed

1/2 cup Asiago cheese, shredded

1 tablespoon Italian seasoning mix

3 tablespoons Romano cheese, grated

1 tablespoon fresh basil leaves, chiffonade

*Directions*

Bring a large pot of lightly salted water to a boil. Cook your spaghetti for 10 minutes or until al dente; drain and reserve, keeping warm.

Stir in the chicken sausage, tomato puree, Asiago cheese, and Italian seasoning mix.

Then, spritz a baking pan with cooking spray; add the spaghetti mixture to the pan. Bake in the preheated Air Fryer at 325 degrees F for 11 minutes.

Top with the grated Romano cheese. Turn the temperature to 390 degrees F and cook an additional 5 minutes or until everything is thoroughly heated and the cheese is melted.

Garnish with fresh basil leaves. Bon appétit!

# Vermouth Bacon and Turkey Burgers

*(Ready in about 30 minutes | Servings 4)*

**Per serving:** 564 Calories; 30.6g Fat; 32.9g Carbs; 37.7g Protein; 11.1g Sugars

*Ingredients*

2 tablespoons vermouth

1 tablespoon honey

2 strips Canadian bacon, sliced

1 pound ground turkey

1/2 shallot, minced

2 garlic cloves, minced

2 tablespoons fish sauce

Sea salt and ground black pepper, to taste

1 teaspoon red pepper flakes
4 soft hamburger rolls
4 tablespoons tomato ketchup
4 tablespoons mayonnaise
4 (1-ounce) slices Cheddar cheese
4 lettuce leaves

*Directions*
Start by preheating your Air Fryer to 400 degrees F.
Whisk the vermouth and honey in a mixing bowl; brush the Canadian bacon with the vermouth mixture.
Cook for 3 minutes. Flip the bacon over and cook an additional 3 minutes.
Then, thoroughly combine the ground turkey, shallots, garlic, fish sauce, salt, black pepper, and red pepper. Form the meat mixture into 4 burger patties.
Bake in the preheated Air Fryer at 370 degrees F for 10 minutes. Flip them over and cook another 10 minutes.
Spread the ketchup and mayonnaise on the inside of the hamburger rolls and place the burgers on the rolls; top with bacon, cheese and lettuce; serve immediately.

# Chicken Taquitos with Homemade Guacamole

*(Ready in about 35 minutes | Servings 4)*
**Per serving:** 512 Calories; 35.2g Fat; 15.9g Carbs; 34.9g Protein; 4.7g Sugars

*Ingredients*
1 tablespoon peanut oil
1 pound chicken breast
Seasoned salt and ground black pepper, to taste
1 teaspoon chili powder
1 teaspoon garlic powder
1 teaspoon ground cumin
1 cup Colby cheese, shredded
8 corn tortillas
1/2 cup sour cream
Guacamole:
1 ripe avocado, pitted and peeled
1 tomato, crushed
1/2 onion, finely chopped
1 tablespoon fresh cilantro, chopped
1 chili pepper, seeded and minced
1 teaspoon fresh garlic, minced
1 lime, juiced
Sea salt and black pepper, to taste

*Directions*
Start by preheating your Air Fryer to 370 degrees F.
Drizzle the peanut oil all over the chicken breast. Then, rub the chicken breast with salt, black pepper, chili powder, garlic powder, and ground cumin.
Cook in the preheated Air Fryer approximately 15 minutes. Turn them over and cook an additional 8 minutes.
Then, increase the temperature to 380 degrees F. Divide the roasted chicken and cheese between tortillas. Now, roll up the tortilla and transfer them to the lightly greased cooking basket. Spritz a nonstick cooking spray over the tortillas.
Cook approximately 10 minutes, turning them over halfway through.
Mash the avocado with a fork and add the remaining ingredients for the guacamole. Serve the chicken taquitos with the guacamole sauce and sour cream. Enjoy!

# Pilaf with Chicken and Beer

*(Ready in about 45 minutes | Servings 4)*

**Per serving:** 529 Calories; 9.6g Fat; 65.5g Carbs; 37.9g Protein; 0.9g Sugars

## Ingredients

1 tablespoon peanut oil

1 ½ cups white rice

5 cups chicken stock

1 cup beer

1 pound chicken tenders

Salt and pepper, to taste

6 tablespoons grated parmesan

## Directions

Preheat your Air Fryer to 350 degrees F. Place the peanut oil in the baking pan and heat it for 1 to 2 minutes. Then, add the rice and cook for 3 minutes until the rice is lightly toasted.

Pour in the chicken stock and beer; cook for 20 minutes. Add the chicken tenders and cook for a further 10 minutes. Season with salt and pepper. Check the rice for doneness. Top with the grated parmesan and cook an additional 5 minutes. Spoon the warm pilaf into individual bowl and serve warm.

# PORK

## Sri Lankan Pork Curry

*(Ready in about 35 minutes | Servings 4)*
**Per serving:** 396 Calories; 20.1g Fat; 4.9g Carbs; 44.2g Protein; 3.6g Sugars

*Ingredients*
2 cardamom pods, only the seeds, crushed
1 teaspoon fennel seeds
1 teaspoon cumin seeds
1 teaspoon coriander seeds
2 teaspoons peanut oil
2 scallions, chopped
2 garlic cloves, smashed
2 jalapeno peppers, minced
1/2 teaspoon ginger, freshly grated
1 pound pork loin, cut into bite-sized cubes
1 cup coconut milk
1 cup chicken broth
1 teaspoon turmeric powder
1 tablespoon tamarind paste
1 tablespoon fresh lime juice

*Directions*
Place the cardamom, fennel, cumin, and coriander seeds in a nonstick skillet over medium-high heat. Stir for 6 minutes until the spices become aromatic and start to brown. Stir frequently to prevent the spices from burning. Set aside.

Preheat your Air Fryer to 370 degrees F. Then, in a baking pan, heat the peanut oil for 2 minutes. Once hot, sauté the scallions for 2 to 3 minutes until tender.

Stir in the garlic, peppers, and ginger; cook an additional minute, stirring frequently. Next, cook the pork for 3 to 4 minutes.

Pour in the coconut milk and broth. Add the reserved seeds, turmeric, and tamarind paste. Let it cook for 15 minutes in the preheated Air Fryer. Divide between individual bowls; drizzle fresh lime juice over the top and serve immediately.

## Herbed and Garlicky Pork Belly

*(Ready in about 1 hour 15 minutes + marinating time | Servings 4)*
**Per serving:** 590 Calories; 60.1g Fat; 0.5g Carbs; 10.6g Protein; 0g Sugars

*Ingredients*
1 pound pork belly
2 garlic cloves, halved
1 teaspoon shallot powder
1 teaspoon sea salt
1 teaspoon dried basil
1 teaspoon dried oregano
1 teaspoon dried thyme
1 teaspoon dried marjoram
1 teaspoon ground black pepper
1 lime, juiced

*Directions*
Blanch the pork belly in a pot of boiling water for 10 to 13 minutes.

Pat it dry with a kitchen towel. Now, poke holes all over the skin by using a fork.

Then, mix the remaining ingredients to make the rub. Massage the rub all over the pork belly. Drizzle lime juice all over the meat; place the pork belly in the refrigerator for 3 hours.

Preheat your Air Fryer to 320 degrees F. Cook the pork belly for 35 minutes.

Turn up the temperature to 360 degrees F and continue cooking for 20 minutes longer. Serve warm. Bon appétit!

# Party Pork and Bacon Skewers

*(Ready in about 30 minutes + marinating time | Servings 6)*

**Per serving:** 572 Calories; 41.1g Fat; 8.9g Carbs; 41.6g Protein; 5.4g Sugars

*Ingredients*

1 cup cream of celery soup

1 (13.5-ounce) can coconut milk, unsweetened

2 tablespoons tamari sauce

1 teaspoon yellow mustard

1 tablespoon honey

Salt and freshly ground white pepper, to taste

1/2 teaspoon cayenne pepper

1/2 teaspoon chili powder

1 teaspoon curry powder

2 pounds pork tenderloin, cut into bite-sized cubes

4 ounces bacon, cut into pieces

12 bamboo skewers, soaked in water

*Directions*

In a large pot, bring the cream of the celery soup, coconut milk, tamari sauce, mustard, honey, salt, white pepper, cayenne pepper, chili powder, and curry powder to a boil.

Then, reduce the heat to simmer; cook until the sauce is heated through, about 13 minutes.

Add the pork, gently stir, and place in your refrigerator for 2 hours.

Thread the pork onto the skewers, alternating the cubes of meat with the pieces of bacon.

Preheat your Air Fryer to 370 degrees F. Cook for 15 minutes, turning over a couple of times. Bon appétit!

# Ranchero Pork Kebabs

*(Ready in about 25 minutes | Servings 3)*

**Per serving:** 394 Calories; 16.7g Fat; 32.9g Carbs; 29.1g Protein; 4.9g Sugars

*Ingredients*

1 pound lean pork, ground

1 onion, chopped

1 garlic clove, smashed

1 teaspoon mustard

Salt and ground black pepper, to taste

4 tablespoons ranch-flavored tortilla chips, finely crushed

*Directions*

Mix all ingredients using your hands. Knead until everything is well incorporated.

Shape the meat mixture around flat skewers (sausage shapes).

Cook at 365 degrees F for 11 to 12 minutes, turning them over once or twice. Work in batches. Serve!

# Pork Stuffed Peppers with Cheese

*(Ready in about 30 minutes | Servings 3)*

**Per serving:** 425 Calories; 25.9g Fat; 9.5g Carbs; 38.3g Protein; 5.2g Sugars

*Ingredients*

3 bell peppers, stems and seeds removed

1 tablespoon olive oil

3 scallions, chopped

1 teaspoon fresh garlic, minced

12 ounces lean pork, ground

1/2 teaspoon sea salt

1/2 teaspoon black pepper

1 tablespoon fish sauce

2 ripe tomatoes, pureed

3 ounces Monterey Jack cheese, grated

*Directions*

Cook the peppers in boiling salted water for 4 minutes

In a nonstick skillet, heat the olive oil over medium heat. Then, sauté the scallions and garlic until tender and fragrant.

Stir in the ground pork and continue sautéing until the pork has browned; drain off the excess fat.

Add the salt, black pepper, fish sauce, and 1 pureed tomato; give it a good stir.

Divide the filling among the bell peppers. Arrange the peppers in a baking dish lightly greased with cooking oil. Place the remaining tomato puree around the peppers.

Bake in the preheated Air Fryer at 380 degrees F for 13 minutes. Top with grated cheese and bake another 6 minutes. Serve warm and enjoy!

# Enchilada Bake with Corn and Cheese

*(Ready in about 30 minutes | Servings 3)*

**Per serving:** 550 Calories; 24.5g Fat; 39g Carbs; 48.3g Protein; 8.7g Sugars

*Ingredients*

1 tablespoon butter, melted

2 scallions, chopped

1 teaspoon fresh garlic, minced

1 pound ground pork

1 tablespoon California chili powder

1 cup tomato sauce

1 cup chicken stock

1/4 teaspoon ground cumin

2 tablespoons fish sauce

3 corn tortillas

1 cup corn

1 cup Colby cheese, shredded

*Directions*

Melt the butter in a saucepan over medium heat. Now, add the scallions and garlic and cook for 2 minutes or until tender.

Add the ground pork and cook for a further 3 minutes, crumbling with a spatula.

To make the enchilada sauce, in a mixing bowl, thoroughly combine the chili powder, tomato sauce, chicken stock, cumin, and fish sauce.

Place little sauce on the bottom of a baking pan. Add one tortilla and 1/3 of the tomato sauce; top with 1/3 of the ground pork mixture. Add 1/3 cup of the corn and 1/3 cup of the shredded Colby cheese.

Repeat these steps 2 more times, finishing with cheese.

Cover the top of the casserole with a piece of foil and place in the cooking basket. Cook for 16 minutes at 250 degrees F. Bon appétit!

# Cracker Pork Chops with Mustard

*(Ready in about 20 minutes | Servings 3)*

**Per serving:** 474 Calories; 19.3g Fat; 10.7g Carbs; 60.2g Protein; 0.5g Sugars

*Ingredients*

1/4 cup all-purpose flour

1 teaspoon turmeric powder

1 egg

1 teaspoon mustard

Kosher salt, to taste

1/4 teaspoon freshly ground black pepper

2 cups crackers, crushed

1/2 teaspoon porcini powder

1 teaspoon shallot powder

3 center-cut loin pork chops

*Directions*

Place the flour and turmeric in a shallow bowl. In another bowl, whisk the eggs, mustard, salt, and black pepper.

In the third bowl, mix the crushed crackers with the porcini powder and shallot powder.

Preheat your Air Fryer to 390 degrees F. Dredge the pork chops in the flour mixture, then in the egg, followed by the cracker mixture.

Cook the pork chops for 7 minutes per side, spraying with cooking oil. Bon appétit!

## Festive Pork Fillets with Apples

*(Ready in about 20 minutes | Servings 3)*

**Per serving:** 485 Calories; 27.3g Fat; 14.7g Carbs; 42.8g Protein; 7.1g Sugars

*Ingredients*

1/4 cup chickpea flour

2 tablespoons Romano cheese, grated

1 teaspoon onion powder

1 teaspoon garlic powder

1/2 teaspoon ground cumin

1 teaspoon cayenne pepper

2 pork fillets (1 pound)

1 Granny Smiths apple, peeled and sliced

1 tablespoon lemon juice

1 ounce butter, cold

*Directions*

Combine the flour, cheese, onions powder, garlic powder, cumin, and cayenne pepper in a ziploc bag; shake to mix well.

Place the pork fillets in the bag. Shake to coat on all sides. Next, spritz the bottom of the Air Fryer basket with cooking spray.

Cook in the preheated Air Fryer at 370 degrees F for 10 minutes. Add the apples and drizzle with lemon juice; place the cold butter on top and cook an additional 5 minutes. Serve immediately.

## Dijon Ribs with Cherry Tomatoes

*(Ready in about 35 minutes | Servings 2)*

**Per serving:** 452 Calories; 17.1g Fat; 17.7g Carbs; 55.2g Protein; 13.6g Sugars

1 rack ribs, cut in half to fit the Air Fryer

1/4 cup dry white wine

2 tablespoons soy sauce

1 tablespoon Dijon mustard

Sea salt and ground black pepper, to taste

1 cup cherry tomatoes

1 teaspoon dried rosemary

*Directions*

Toss the pork ribs with wine, soy sauce, mustard, salt, and black pepper.

Add the ribs to the lightly greased cooking basket. Cook in the preheated Air Fryer at 370 degrees F for 25 minutes.

Turn the ribs over, add the cherry tomatoes and rosemary; cook an additional 5 minutes. Serve immediately.

## Pork Cutlets with Plum Sauce

*(Ready in about 20 minutes | Servings 4)*

**Per serving:** 422 Calories; 23.8g Fat; 20.8g Carbs; 29.4g Protein; 18.3g Sugars

*Ingredients*

4 pork cutlets

2 teaspoons sesame oil

1/2 teaspoon ground black pepper

Salt, to taste

1 tablespoon Creole seasoning

2 tablespoons aged balsamic vinegar

2 tablespoons soy sauce

6 ripe plums, pitted and diced

*Directions*

Preheat your Air Fryer to 390 degrees F.

Toss the pork cutlets with the sesame oil, black pepper, salt, Creole seasoning, vinegar, and soy sauce. Transfer them to a lightly greased baking pan; lower the pan onto the cooking basket.

Cook for 13 minutes in the preheated Air Fryer, flipping them halfway through the cooking time. Serve warm.

## Hawaiian Cheesy Meatball Sliders

*(Ready in about 20 minutes | Servings 4)*

**Per serving:** 612 Calories; 34.9g Fat; 39.4g Carbs; 33.3g Protein; 10.8g Sugars

*Ingredients*

1 pound ground pork

2 tablespoons bacon, chopped

2 garlic cloves, minced

2 tablespoons scallions, chopped

Salt and ground black pepper, to taste

1/2 cup Romano cheese, grated

1 cup tortilla chips, crushed

1 ½ cups marinara sauce

8 Hawaiian rolls

1 cup Cheddar cheese, shredded

*Directions*

Mix the ground pork with the bacon, garlic, scallions, salt, black pepper, cheese, and tortilla chips. Shape the mixture into 8 meatballs.

Add the meatballs to the lightly greased baking pan. Pour in the marinara sauce and lower the pan onto the cooking basket.

Cook the meatballs in the preheated Air Fryer at 380 degrees for 10 minutes. Check the meatballs halfway through the cooking time.

Place one meatball on top of the bottom half of one roll. Spoon the marinara sauce on top of each meatball. Top with cheese and bake in your Air Fryer at 370 degrees F for 3 to 4 minutes.

Top with the other half of the roll and serve immediately. Bon appétit!

## Country-Style Pork and Mushroom Patties

*(Ready in about 30 minutes | Servings 4)*

**Per serving:** 399 Calories; 29.7g Fat; 8.7g Carbs; 24.3g Protein; 4.6g Sugars

*Ingredients*

1 tablespoon canola oil

1 onion, chopped

2 garlic cloves, minced

1 pound ground pork

1/2 pound brown mushrooms, chopped

Salt and black pepper, to taste

1 teaspoon cayenne pepper

1/2 teaspoon dried rosemary

1/2 teaspoon dried dill

4 slices Cheddar cheese

*Directions*

Start by preheating your Air Fryer to 370 degrees F.

In a mixing bowl, thoroughly combine the oil, onions, garlic, ground pork, mushrooms, salt, black pepper, cayenne pepper, rosemary, and dill. Shape the meat mixture into four patties.

Spritz the bottom of the cooking basket with cooking spray. Cook the meatballs in the preheated Air Fryer at 370 degrees for 20 minutes, flipping them halfway through cooking. Top the warm patties with cheese and serve. Enjoy!

# Meatloaf Muffins with Sweet Potato Frosting

*(Ready in about 1 hour | Servings 4)*

**Per serving:** 408 Calories; 23.4g Fat; 32.7g Carbs; 21.7g Protein; 7.1g Sugars

*Ingredients*

Meatloaf Muffins:

1 pound pork sausage, crumbled

1 shallot, chopped

2 garlic cloves, minced

1/2 cup oats

1/2 cup pasta sauce

1 teaspoon dried oregano

1 teaspoon dried basil

Salt and ground black pepper, to taste

1 egg

Sweet Potato Frosting:

1/2 pound sweet potatoes, cut into wedges

1/2 teaspoon garlic powder

1/4 cup coconut milk

1 tablespoon coconut oil

1 teaspoon salt

*Directions*

Mix all ingredients for the meatloaf muffins until everything is well incorporated.

Place the meat mixture in 4 cupcake liners. Bake at 220 degrees F for 23 minutes. Remove from the cooking basket and reserve keeping warm.

Cook the sweet potatoes at 380 degrees F for 35 minutes, shaking the basket occasionally. When the sweet potatoes are cooled enough to handle, scoop out the flesh into a bowl.

Add the garlic powder, coconut milk, coconut oil, and salt; mix to combine well. Beat with a wire whisk until everything is thoroughly mixed and fluffy.

Pipe the potato mixture onto the sausage muffins using a pastry bag. Enjoy!

# Japanese Ribs (Supearibu no Nikomi)

*(Ready in about 25 minutes | Servings 4)*

**Per serving:** 506 Calories; 28.1g Fat; 16.8g Carbs; 45.2g Protein; 12.3g Sugars

*Ingredients*

2 pounds pork ribs

1/2 cup tomato puree

1/2 cup ketchup

1 teaspoon orange zest

1 tablespoon Worcestershire sauce

2 tablespoons brown sugar

1 teaspoon garlic powder

1 tablespoon instant dashi

1 tablespoon mirin

1 tablespoon black sesame seeds

*Directions*

Preheat your Air Fryer to 370 degrees F.

Toss the pork ribs with all ingredients, except the sesame seeds, in a nonstick grill pan.

Grill your ribs approximately 18 minutes at 390 degrees F, turning them periodically.

Serve with the sauce and black sesame seeds and enjoy!

# Elegant Pork Chops with Applesauce

*(Ready in about 20 minutes | Servings 4)*

**Per serving:** 427 Calories; 21.1g Fat; 17.6g Carbs; 40.7g Protein; 14.3g Sugars

*Ingredients*

4 pork chops, bone-in

Sea salt and ground black pepper, to taste

1/2 teaspoon onion powder

1/2 teaspoon paprika

1/2 teaspoon celery seeds

2 cooking apples, peeled and sliced

1 tablespoon honey

1 tablespoon peanut oil

*Directions*

Place the pork in a lightly greased baking pan. Season with salt and pepper, and transfer the pan to the cooking basket.

Cook in the preheated Air Fryer at 370 degrees F for 10 minutes.

Meanwhile, in a saucepan, simmer the remaining ingredients over medium heat for about 8 minutes or until the apples are softened.

Pour the applesauce over the prepared pork chops. Add to the Air Fryer and bake for 5 minutes more. Bon appétit!

## Easy Minty Meatballs

*(Ready in about 20 minutes | Servings 4)*

**Per serving:** 311 Calories; 19.5g Fat; 3.5g Carbs; 30.1g Protein; 1.3g Sugars

*Ingredients*

1/2 pound ground pork

1/2 pound ground beef

1 shallot, chopped

2 garlic cloves, minced

1 tablespoon coriander, chopped

1 teaspoon fresh mint, minced

Sea salt and ground black pepper, to taste

1/2 teaspoon mustard seeds

1 teaspoon fennel seeds

1 teaspoon ground cumin

1 cup mozzarella, sliced

*Directions*

In a mixing bowl, combine all ingredients, except the mozzarella.

Shape the mixture into balls and transfer them to a lightly greased cooking basket.

Cook the meatballs in the preheated Air Fryer at 380 degrees for 10 minutes. Check the meatballs halfway through the cooking time.

Top with sliced mozzarella and bake for 3 minutes more. To serve, arrange on a nice serving platter. Bon appétit!

## Spanish-Style Pork with Padrón Peppers

*(Ready in about 30 minutes | Servings 4)*

**Per serving:** 536 Calories; 29.5g Fat; 5.9g Carbs; 59g Protein; 2.9g Sugars

*Ingredients*

1 tablespoon olive oil

8 ounces Padrón peppers

2 pounds pork loin, sliced

1 teaspoon Celtic salt

1 teaspoon paprika

1 heaped tablespoon capers, drained

8 green olives, pitted and halved

*Directions*

Drizzle olive oil all over the Padrón peppers; cook them in the preheated Air Fryer at 400 degrees F for 10 minutes, turning occasionally, until well blistered all over and tender-crisp.

Then, turn the temperature to 360 degrees F. Season the pork loin with salt and paprika. Add the capers and cook for 16 minutes, turning them over halfway through the cooking time. Serve with olives and the reserved Padrón peppers.

# Italian Sausage Meatball Casserole

*(Ready in about 35 minutes | Servings 4)*
**Per serving:** 534 Calories; 29.7g Fat; 46g Carbs; 23.1g Protein; 8.1g Sugars

*Ingredients*
1 pound Italian pork sausage, crumbled
1 egg
1 cup regular rolled oat
1 teaspoon cayenne pepper
Sea salt and ground black pepper, to taste
1 tablespoon olive oil
1 leek, chopped
1 teaspoon fresh garlic, minced
1 chili pepper, chopped
1 teaspoon dried oregano
1 teaspoon dried basil
1 teaspoon celery seeds
1 teaspoon brown mustard
2 cups tomato puree

*Directions*
In a mixing bowl, thoroughly combine the pork sausage with egg, oats, cayenne pepper, salt, and black pepper. Form the sausage mixture into meatballs.

Spritz the Air Fryer basket with cooking oil. Cook the meatballs in the preheated Air Fryer at 380 degrees for 10 minutes, shaking the basket halfway through the cooking time. Reserve.

Meanwhile, heat the olive oil in a pan over medium-high heat. Sauté the leeks until tender and aromatic.

Stir in the garlic, pepper, and seasonings and cook for a further 2 minutes. Add the brown mustard and tomato puree and cook another 5 minutes.

Transfer the tomato sauce to the baking pan. Add the meatballs and cook in the preheated Air Fryer at 350 degrees F for 10 minutes. Serve warm.

# Omelet with Prosciutto and Ricotta Cheese

*(Ready in about 15 minutes | Servings 2)*
**Per serving:** 389 Calories; 28.8g Fat; 3.2g Carbs; 29.1g Protein; 0.5g Sugars

*Ingredients*
2 tablespoons olive oil
4 eggs
2 tablespoons scallions, chopped
4 tablespoons Ricotta cheese
1/4 teaspoon black pepper, freshly cracked
Salt, to taste
6 ounces prosciutto, chopped
1 tablespoon Italian parsley, roughly chopped

*Directions*
Generously grease a baking pan with olive oil. Then, whisk the eggs, and add the scallions, cheese, black pepper, and salt. Fold in the chopped prosciutto and mix to combine well. Spoon into the prepared baking pan.

Cook in the preheated Air Fryer at 360 F for 6 minutes. Serve immediately garnished with Italian parsley.

# Pigs in a Blanket with a Twist

*(Ready in about 15 minutes | Servings 4)*
**Per serving:** 589 Calories; 40g Fat; 40.1g Carbs; 16.8g Protein; 7g Sugars

*Ingredients*
12 refrigerator biscuits
8 hot dogs, cut into 3 pieces
1 egg yolk

2 tablespoons poppy seeds

1 tablespoon oregano

*Directions*

Flatten each biscuit slightly; cut in half.

Now, mix the egg yolk with the poppy seeds and oregano.

Wrap the biscuits around the hot dog pieces sealing the edges and brushing with the egg mixture to adhere.

Bake in the preheated Air Fryer at 395 degrees F for 8 minutes, Enjoy!

# Tagliatelle al Ragu

*(Ready in about 30 minutes | Servings 4)*

**Per serving:** 522 Calories; 32.2g Fat; 35.8g Carbs; 22.2g Protein; 4.2g Sugars

*Ingredients*

1 tablespoon olive oil

1 shallot, chopped

2 garlic cloves, minced

2 bell peppers, sliced

1 carrot, trimmed and sliced

1/2 pound ground pork

1/2 pound smoked pork sausage, sliced

2 ripe medium-sized tomatoes, pureed

2 tablespoons ketchup

1/4 cup red wine

2 tablespoons cilantro leaves, chopped

1 teaspoon dried basil

1 teaspoon dried oregano

Salt and ground black pepper, to taste

1 package (16-ounce) tagliatelle

*Directions*

Heat the oil in the baking pan at 380 degrees F. Then, sauté the shallots until tender about 4 minutes.

Add the garlic, bell pepper, and carrots; cook an additional 2 minutes.

Now, stir in ground pork and sausage and continue cooking for 5 minutes more, crumbling the meat with a spatula.

Add tomato puree, ketchup, red wine, cilantro, basil, oregano, salt, and black pepper. Then, cook for 4 to 6 minutes longer or until everything is heated through.

Meanwhile, bring a large pot of lightly salted water to a boil. Cook your tagliatelle for 10 to 12 minutes; drain.

Top tagliatelle with the sauce and serve. Bon appétit!

# Filipino Pork Adobo

*(Ready in about 35 minutes | Servings 4)*

**Per serving:** 334 Calories; 16.8g Fat; 12.8g Carbs; 33.6g Protein; 6.1g Sugars

*Ingredients*

1 tablespoon sesame oil

1 ½ pounds Boston butt, boneless and skinless, cut into 2 pieces

Sea salt and ground black pepper, to taste

1 teaspoon paprika

1/2 teaspoon mustard seeds

1 teaspoon sesame oil

3 bell peppers, seeded and sliced

1 jalapeño pepper, seeded and sliced

1 red onion, sliced

2 garlic cloves, smashed

1/2 teaspoon curry

1/2 teaspoon ground bay leaf

1/4 cup soy sauce

1/4 cup apple cider vinegar

1 tablespoon cornstarch plus 2 tablespoons water

*Directions*

Rub 1 tablespoon of sesame oil all over the Boston butt. Season with salt, pepper, paprika, and mustard seeds.

Roast the Boston butt in the preheated Air Fryer at 390 degrees F for 10 minutes. Turn them over and cook another 10 minutes.

Heat 1 teaspoon of sesame oil in a wok over medium-high heat. Once hot, cook the peppers until tender, about 2 minutes.

Add the onion, garlic, curry, bay leaf, soy sauce, and vinegar. Cook an additional 5 minutes, stirring frequently.

Add the cornstarch slurry and meat. Reduce the temperature to simmer and cook for 2 to 4 minute more or until everything is thoroughly heated. Bon appétit!

## Spanish Pork Skewers (Pinchos Morunos)

*(Ready in about 35 minutes + marinating time | Servings 4)*

**Per serving:** 432 Calories; 23g Fat; 3.4g Carbs; 49.4g Protein; 0.4g Sugars

### Ingredients

2 pounds center cut loin chop, cut into bite-sized pieces
1 teaspoon oregano
1/2 teaspoon ground turmeric
1/2 teaspoon ground coriander
1 teaspoon ground cumin
2 teaspoons sweet Spanish paprika
Sea salt and freshly ground black pepper, to taste
2 garlic cloves, minced
2 tablespoons extra virgin olive oil
1/4 cup dry red wine
1 lemon, 1/2 juiced 1/2 wedges

### Directions

Mix all ingredients, except the lemon wedges, in a large ceramic dish. Allow it to marinate for 2 hours in your refrigerator.

Discard the marinade. Now, thread the pork pieces on to skewers and place them in the cooking basket.

Cook in the preheated Air Fryer at 360 degrees F for 15 to 17 minutes, shaking the basket every 5 minutes. Work in batches.

Serve immediately garnished with lemon wedges. Bon appétit!

## Greek Pork Loin with Tzatziki

*(Ready in about 55 minutes | Servings 4)*

**Per serving:** 560 Calories; 30.1g Fat; 4.9g Carbs; 64.1g Protein; 1.6g Sugars

### Ingredients

Greek Pork:
2 pounds pork sirloin roast
Salt and black pepper, to taste
1 teaspoon smoked paprika
1/2 teaspoon mustard seeds
1/2 teaspoon celery seeds
1 teaspoon fennel seeds
1 teaspoon Ancho chili powder
1 teaspoon turmeric powder
1/2 teaspoon ground ginger
2 tablespoons olive oil
2 cloves garlic, finely chopped
Tzatziki:
1/2 cucumber, finely chopped and squeezed
1 cup full-fat Greek yogurt
1 garlic clove, minced
1 tablespoon extra virgin olive oil
1 teaspoon balsamic vinegar
1 teaspoon minced fresh dill
A pinch of salt

### Directions

Toss all ingredients for Greek pork in a large mixing bowl. Toss until the meat is well coated.

Cook in the preheated Air Fryer at 360 degrees F for 30 minutes; turn over and cook another 20 minutes.

Meanwhile, prepare the tzatziki by mixing all the tzatziki ingredients. Place in your refrigerator until ready to use.

Serve the pork sirloin roast with the chilled tzatziki on the side. Enjoy!

# Pork Ragout with Egg Noodles

*(Ready in about 50 minutes | Servings 4)*

**Per serving:** 615 Calories; 20.8g Fat; 44.2g Carbs; 59g Protein; 3.2g Sugars

*Ingredients*

2 pounds country pork ribs

Sea salt, to your liking

1/2 teaspoon freshly cracked black pepper

1/2 teaspoon cayenne pepper

1 tablespoon yellow mustard

2 tablespoons sesame oil

1 shallot, diced

2 ripe tomatoes, pureed

1 cup vegetable broth

1/4 cup red wine

1 tablespoon fish sauce

1 tablespoon fresh lemon juice

1 teaspoon dried thyme

2 bay leaves

8 ounces egg noodles

*Directions*

Place all ingredients, except the egg noodles, in a ceramic bowl; let it marinate at least 1 hour in your refrigerator.

Discard the marinade and place the pork ribs in the lightly greased cooking basket.

Cook at 365 degrees for 17 minutes. Turn the ribs over and cook an additional 14 to 15 minutes; reserve.

Meanwhile, bring a large pot of lightly salted water to a boil. Cook the egg noodles for 10 to 12 minutes; drain and reserve, keeping warm.

Then, heat the reserved marinade in a large nonstick skillet over a moderate flame; simmer the marinade for 5 to 7 minutes or until it has reduced by half.

Add in the reserved meat and egg noodles; let it simmer an additional 3 to 4 minutes or until thoroughly heated. Bon appétit!

# Porterhouse Steak for Two

*(Ready in about 25 minutes | Servings 2)*

**Per serving:** 402 Calories; 14.6g Fat; 0.1g Carbs; 67.2g Protein; 0g Sugars

*Ingredients*

1 pound porterhouse steak, cut meat from bone in 2 pieces

1/2 teaspoon ground black pepper

1 teaspoon cayenne pepper

1/2 teaspoon salt

1 teaspoon garlic powder

1/2 teaspoon dried thyme

1/2 teaspoon dried marjoram

1 teaspoon Dijon mustard

1 tablespoon butter, melted

*Directions*

Sprinkle the porterhouse steak with all the seasonings.

Spread the mustard and butter evenly over the meat.

Cook in the preheated Air Fryer at 390 degrees F for 12 to 14 minutes.

Taste for doneness with a meat thermometer and serve immediately.

# Pork Leg with Candy Onions

*(Ready in about 1 hour | Servings 4)*

**Per serving:** 444 Calories; 12.8g Fat; 11.6g Carbs; 67g Protein; 6.8g Sugars

*Ingredients*

1 rosemary sprig, chopped

1 thyme sprig, chopped

1 teaspoon dried sage, crushed

Sea salt and ground black pepper, to taste

1 teaspoon cayenne pepper

2 teaspoons sesame oil

2 pounds pork leg roast, scored

1 pound candy onions, peeled

2 chili peppers, minced

4 cloves garlic, finely chopped

*Directions*

Start by preheating your Air Fryer to 400 degrees F.

Then, mix the seasonings with the sesame oil. Rub the seasoning mixture all over the pork leg. Cook in the preheated Air Fryer for 40 minutes. Add the candy onions, peppers and garlic and cook an additional 12 minutes. Slice the pork leg. Afterwards, spoon the pan juices over the meat and serve with the candy onions. Bon appétit!

# Taco Casserole with Cheese

*(Ready in about 25 minutes | Servings 4)*

**Per serving:** 449 Calories; 23g Fat; 5.6g Carbs; 54g Protein; 3.2g Sugars

*Ingredients*

1 pound lean ground pork

1/2 pound ground beef

1/4 cup tomato puree

Sea salt and ground black pepper, to taste

1 teaspoon smoked paprika

1/2 teaspoon dried oregano

1 teaspoon dried basil

1 teaspoon dried rosemary

2 eggs

1 cup Cottage cheese, crumbled, at room temperature

1/2 cup Cotija cheese, shredded

*Directions*

Lightly grease a casserole dish with a nonstick cooking oil. Add the ground meat to the bottom of your casserole dish.

Add the tomato puree. Sprinkle with salt, black pepper, paprika, oregano, basil, and rosemary.

In a mixing bowl, whisk the egg with cheese. Place on top of the ground meat mixture. Place a piece of foil on top.

Bake in the preheated Air Fryer at 350 degrees F for 10 minutes; remove the foil and cook an additional 6 minutes. Bon appétit!

# BEEF

## Easy Asian Gyudon

*(Ready in about 20 minutes | Servings 4)*
**Per serving:** 377 Calories; 32.2g Fat; 3.2g Carbs; 18.5g Protein; 1.9g Sugars

*Ingredients*

1 shallot, chopped

1/2 cup dashi

1 tablespoon mirin

1 teaspoon agave syrup

2 tablespoons Shoyu sauce

1/2 teaspoon wasabi

1 pound rib eye, sliced

*Directions*

Add all ingredients to a lightly greased baking pan. Gently stir to combine.

Cook in the preheated Air Fryer at 400 degrees F for 7 minutes. Stir again and cook for a further 7 minutes.

Serve with Japanese ramen noodles if desired. Enjoy!

## Korean Beef Bowl with Rice

*(Ready in about 20 minutes | Servings 4)*
**Per serving:** 465 Calories; 14.7g Fat; 44.5g Carbs; 37.8g Protein; 1.4g Sugars

*Ingredients*

2 tablespoons bacon, chopped

1 ½ pounds ground chuck

1 leek, chopped

2 garlic cloves, minced

1 tablespoon daenjang (soybean paste)

1 teaspoon kochukaru (chili pepper flakes)

Sea salt and ground black pepper, to taste

2 cups white rice, hot cooked

*Directions*

Start by preheating your Air Fryer to 360 degrees. Then, add the bacon to the baking pan; cook the bacon just until it starts to get crisp.

Add the ground chuck and cook for 2 minutes more, crumbling with a spatula.

Add the leeks, garlic, and spices. Cook for 12 minutes more. Stir in the hot rice; stir well to combine and serve. Enjoy!

## Best Pretzel Sliders

*(Ready in about 40 minutes | Servings 4)*
**Per serving:** 553 Calories; 22.1g Fat; 51.1g Carbs; 37.5g Protein; 8.1g Sugars

*Ingredients*

3/4 pound ground beef

1 smoked beef sausage, chopped

4 scallions, chopped

1 garlic clove, minced

2 tablespoons fresh coriander, chopped

4 tablespoons rolled oats

2 tablespoons tomato paste

Himalayan salt and ground black pepper, to taste

8 small pretzel rolls

4 tablespoons mayonnaise

8 thin slices of tomato

*Directions*

Start by preheating your Air Fryer to 370 degrees F.

In a mixing bowl, thoroughly combine the ground beef, sausage, scallions, garlic, coriander, oats, tomato paste, salt, and black pepper. Knead with your hands until everything is well combined.

Form the mixture into eight patties and cook them for 18 to 20 minutes. Work in batches.

Place the burgers on slider buns; top with mayonnaise and tomato slices. Bon appétit!

## Juicy Strip Steak

*(Ready in about 30 minutes | Servings 4)*

**Per serving:** 417 Calories; 17.9g Fat; 15.6g Carbs; 49.1g Protein; 10.1g Sugars

### Ingredients

1 ½ pounds strip steak, sliced

1/4 cup chickpea flour

1/3 cup Shoyu sauce

2 tablespoons honey

1 teaspoon mustard seeds

2 tablespoons champagne vinegar

1 teaspoon ginger-garlic paste

1/2 teaspoon coriander seeds

1 tablespoon cornstarch

### Directions

Start by preheating your Air Fryer to 395 degrees F. Spritz the Air Fryer basket with cooking oil.

Toss the strip steak with chickpea flour. Cook the strip steak for 12 minutes; flip them over and cook an additional 10 minutes.

In the meantime, heat the saucepan over medium-high heat. Add the Shoyu sauce, honey, mustard seeds, champagne vinegar, ginger-garlic paste, and coriander seeds.

Reduce the heat and simmer until the sauce is heated through. Make the slurry by whisking the cornstarch with 1 tablespoon of water.

Now, whisk in the cornstarch slurry and continue to simmer until the sauce has thickened. Spoon the sauce over the steak and serve.

## Birthday Party Cheeseburger Pizza

*(Ready in about 20 minutes | Servings 4)*

**Per serving:** 447 Calories; 16.1g Fat; 29.5g Carbs; 44.5g Protein; 2.7g Sugars

### Ingredients

Nonstick cooking oil

1 pound ground beef

Kosher salt and ground black pepper, to taste

1/2 teaspoon oregano

1/2 teaspoon basil

1/4 teaspoon red pepper flakes

1/4 cup marinara sauce

2 spring onions, chopped

4 burger buns

1 cup mozzarella cheese, shredded

### Directions

Start by preheating your Air Fryer to 370 degrees F. Spritz the Air Fryer basket with cooking oil.

Add the ground beef and cook for 10 minutes, crumbling with a spatula. Season with salt, black pepper, oregano, basil, and red peppers.

Spread the marinara pasta on each half of burger bun. Place the spring onions and ground meat mixture on the buns equally.

Set the temperature to 350 degrees F. Place the burger pizza in the Air Fryer basket. Top with mozzarella cheese.

Bake approximately 4 minutes or until cheese is bubbling. Top with another half of burger bun and serve. Bon appétit!

# Filipino Tortang Giniling

*(Ready in about 20 minutes | Servings 3)*
**Per serving:** 543 Calories; 34.7g Fat; 7.4g Carbs; 48.3g Protein; 4.4g Sugars

*Ingredients*

1 teaspoon lard

2/3 pound ground beef

1/4 teaspoon chili powder

1/2 teaspoon ground bay leaf

1/2 teaspoon ground pepper

Sea salt, to taste

1 green bell pepper, seeded and chopped

1 red bell pepper, seeded and chopped

6 eggs

1/3 cup double cream

1/2 cup Colby cheese, shredded

1 tomato, sliced

*Directions*

Melt the lard in a cast-iron skillet over medium-high heat. Add the ground beef and cook for 4 minutes until no longer pink, crumbling with a spatula.

Add the ground beef mixture, along with the spices to the baking pan. Now, add the bell peppers.

In a mixing bowl, whisk the eggs with double cream. Spoon the mixture over the meat and peppers in the pan.

Cook in the preheated Air Fryer at 355 degrees F for 10 minutes.

Top with the cheese and tomato slices. Continue to cook for 5 minutes more or until the eggs are golden and the cheese has melted.

# Pastrami and Cheddar Quiche

*(Ready in about 20 minutes | Servings 2)*
**Per serving:** 435 Calories; 31.4g Fat; 6.7g Carbs; 30.4g Protein; 3.8g Sugars

*Ingredients*

4 eggs

1 bell pepper, chopped

2 spring onions, chopped

1 cup pastrami, sliced

1/4 cup Greek-style yogurt

1/2 cup Cheddar cheese, grated

Sea salt, to taste

1/4 teaspoon ground black pepper

*Directions*

Start by preheating your Air Fryer to 330 degrees F. Spritz the baking pan with cooking oil.

Then, thoroughly combine all ingredients and pour the mixture into the prepared baking pan.

Cook for 7 to 9 minutes or until the eggs have set. Place on a cooling rack and let it sit for 10 minutes before slicing and serving.

# Roasted Blade Steak with Green Beans

*(Ready in about 25 minutes | Servings 4)*
**Per serving:** 379 Calories; 18.1g Fat; 5.3g Carbs; 49g Protein; 1.9g Sugars

*Ingredients*

2 garlic cloves, smashed

2 teaspoons sunflower oil

1/2 teaspoon cayenne pepper

1 tablespoon Cajun seasoning

1 ½ pounds blade steak

2 cups green beans

1/2 teaspoon Tabasco pepper sauce

Sea salt and ground black pepper, to taste

*Directions*

Start by preheating your Air Fryer to 330 degrees F.

Mix the garlic, oil, cayenne pepper, and Cajun seasoning to make a paste. Rub it over both sides of the blade steak.

Cook for 13 minutes in the preheated Air Fryer. Now, flip the steak and cook an additional 8 minutes.

Heat the green beans in a saucepan. Add a few tablespoons of water, Tabasco, salt, and black pepper; heat until it wilts or about 10 minutes.

Serve the roasted blade steak with green beans on the side. Bon appétit!

## Minty Tender Filet Mignon

*(Ready in about 20 minutes + marinating time | Servings 4)*

**Per serving:** 389 Calories; 20.4g Fat; 4.6g Carbs; 47.3g Protein; 1.7g Sugars

### Ingredients

2 tablespoons olive oil

2 tablespoons Worcestershire sauce

1 lemon, juiced

1/4 cup fresh mint leaves, chopped

4 cloves garlic, minced

Sea salt and ground black pepper, to taste

2 pounds filet mignon

### Directions

In a ceramic bowl, place the olive oil, Worcestershire sauce, lemon juice, mint leaves, garlic, salt, black pepper, and cayenne pepper.

Add the fillet mignon and let it marinate for 2 hours in the refrigerator.

Roast in the preheated Air Fryer at 400 degrees F for 18 minutes, basting with the reserved marinade and flipping a couple of times. Serve warm. Bon appétit!

## Hungarian Oven Stew (Marha Pörkölt)

*(Ready in about 1 hour 10 minutes | Servings 4)*

**Per serving:** 375 Calories; 16.1g Fat; 16.5g Carbs; 39.6g Protein; 4.6g Sugars

### Ingredients

4 tablespoons all-purpose flour

Sea salt and cracked black pepper, to taste

1 teaspoon Hungarian paprika

1 pound beef chuck roast, boneless, cut into bite-sized cubes

2 teaspoons sunflower oil

1 medium-sized leek, chopped

2 garlic cloves, minced

2 bay leaves

1 teaspoon caraway seeds.

2 cups roasted vegetable broth

2 ripe tomatoes, pureed

2 tablespoons red wine

2 bell peppers, chopped

2 medium carrots, sliced

1 celery stalk, peeled and diced

### Directions

Add the flour, salt, black pepper, paprika, and beef to a resealable bag; shake to coat well.

Heat the oil in a Dutch oven over medium-high flame; sauté the leeks, garlic, bay leaves, and caraway seeds about 4 minutes or until fragrant. Transfer to a lightly greased baking pan.

Then, brown the beef, stirring occasionally, working in batches. Add to the baking pan.

Add the vegetable broth, tomatoes, and red wine. Lower the pan onto the Air Fryer basket. Bake at 325 degrees F for 40 minutes.

Add the bell peppers, carrots, and celery. Cook an additional 20 minutes. Serve immediately and enjoy!

# Easy Beef Jerky

*(Ready in about 1 hour + marinating time | Servings 4)*

**Per serving:** 284 Calories; 13.8g Fat; 16.5g Carbs; 23.1g Protein; 11g Sugars

*Ingredients*

1 cup beer

1/2 cup tamari sauce

1 teaspoon liquid smoke

2 garlic cloves, minced

Sea salt and ground black pepper

1 teaspoon ancho chili powder

2 tablespoons honey

3/4 pound flank steak, slice into strips

*Directions*

Place all ingredients in a ceramic dish; let it marinate for 3 hours in the refrigerator. Slice the beef into thin strips

Marinate the beef in the refrigerator overnight.

Now, discard the marinade and hang the meat in the cooking basket by using skewers.

Air Fry at 190 degrees F degrees for 1 hour. Store it in an airtight container for up to 2 weeks.

# Polish Sausage and Sourdough Kabobs

*(Ready in about 20 minutes | Servings 4)*

**Per serving:** 284 Calories; 13.8g Fat; 16.5g Carbs; 23.1g Protein; 11g Sugars

*Ingredients*

1 pound smoked Polish beef sausage, sliced

1 tablespoon mustard

1 tablespoon olive oil

2 tablespoons Worcestershire sauce

2 bell peppers, sliced

2 cups sourdough bread, cubed

Salt and ground black pepper, to taste

*Directions*

Toss the sausage with the mustard, olive, and Worcestershire sauce. Thread sausage, peppers, and bread onto skewers.

Sprinkle with salt and black pepper.

Cook in the preheated Air Fryer at 360 degrees F for 11 minutes. Brush the skewers with the reserved marinade. Bon appétit!

# Ranch Meatloaf with Peppers

*(Ready in about 35 minutes | Servings 5)*

**Per serving:** 411 Calories; 31.4g Fat; 10g Carbs; 28.2g Protein; 4.3g Sugars

*Ingredients*

1 pound beef, ground

1/2 pound veal, ground

1 egg

4 tablespoons vegetable juice

1 cup crackers, crushed

2 bell peppers, chopped

1 onion, chopped

2 garlic cloves, minced

2 tablespoons tomato paste

2 tablespoons soy sauce

1 (1-ounce) package ranch dressing mix

Sea salt, to taste

1/2 teaspoon ground black pepper, to taste

7 ounces tomato paste

1 tablespoon Dijon mustard

*Directions*

Start by preheating your Air Fryer to 330 degrees F.

In a mixing bowl, thoroughly combine the ground beef, veal, egg, vegetable juice, crackers, bell peppers, onion, garlic, tomato paste, soy sauce, ranch dressing mix, salt, and ground black pepper.

Mix until everything is well incorporated and press into a lightly greased meatloaf pan.

Cook approximately 25 minutes in the preheated Air Fryer. Whisk the tomato paste with the mustard and spread the topping over the top of your meatloaf.

Continue to cook 2 minutes more. Let it stand on a cooling rack for 6 minutes before slicing and serving. Enjoy!

## Indian Beef Samosas

*(Ready in about 35 minutes | Servings 8)*

**Per serving:** 266 Calories; 13g Fat; 24.5g Carbs; 12.2g Protein; 1.5g Sugars

### Ingredients

1 tablespoon sesame oil

4 tablespoons shallots, minced

2 cloves garlic, minced

2 tablespoons green chili peppers, chopped

1/2 pound ground chuck

4 ounces bacon, chopped

Salt and ground black pepper, to taste

1 teaspoon cumin powder

1 teaspoon turmeric

1 teaspoon coriander

1 cup frozen peas, thawed

1 (16-ounce) package phyllo dough

1 egg, beaten with 2 tablespoons of water (egg wash)

### Directions

Heat the oil in a saucepan over medium-high heat. Once hot, sauté the shallots, garlic, and chili peppers until tender, about 3 minutes.

Then, add the beef and bacon; continue to sauté an additional 4 minutes, crumbling with a fork. Season with the salt, pepper, cumin powder, turmeric, and coriander. Stir in peas.

Then, preheat your Air Fryer to 330 degrees F. Brush the Air Fryer basket with cooking oil.

Place 1 to 2 tablespoons of the mixture onto each phyllo sheet. Fold the sheets into triangles, pressing the edges. Brush the tops with egg wash. Bake for 7 to 8 minutes, working with batches. Serve with Indian tomato sauce if desired. Enjoy!

## Grilled Vienna Sausage with Broccoli

*(Ready in about 25 minutes | Servings 4)*

**Per serving:** 477 Calories; 43.2g Fat; 7.3g Carbs; 15.9g Protein; 0.7g Sugars

### Ingredients

1 pound beef Vienna sausage

1/2 cup mayonnaise

1 teaspoon yellow mustard

1 tablespoon fresh lemon juice

1 teaspoon garlic powder

1/4 teaspoon black pepper

1 pound broccoli

### Directions

Start by preheating your Air Fryer to 380 degrees F. Spritz the grill pan with cooking oil.

Cut the sausages into serving sized pieces. Cook the sausages for 15 minutes, shaking the basket occasionally to get all sides browned. Set aside.

In the meantime, whisk the mayonnaise with mustard, lemon juice, garlic powder, and black pepper. Toss the broccoli with the mayo mixture. Turn up temperature to 400 degrees F. Cook broccoli for 6 minutes, turning halfway through the cooking time.

Serve the sausage with the grilled broccoli on the side. Bon appétit!

# Aromatic T-Bone Steak with Garlic

*(Ready in about 20 minutes | Servings 3)*
**Per serving:** 463 Calories; 24.6g Fat; 16.7g Carbs; 44.7g Protein; 5.2g Sugars

*Ingredients*

1 pound T-bone steak

4 garlic cloves, halved

1/4 cup all-purpose flour

2 tablespoons olive oil

1/4 cup tamari sauce

2 teaspoons brown sugar

4 tablespoons tomato paste

1 teaspoon Sriracha sauce

2 tablespoons white vinegar

1 teaspoon dried rosemary

1/2 teaspoon dried basil

2 heaping tablespoons cilantro, chopped

*Directions*

Rub the garlic halves all over the T-bone steak. Toss the steak with the flour.

Drizzle the oil all over the steak and transfer it to the grill pan; grill the steak in the preheated Air Fryer at 400 degrees F for 10 minutes.

Meanwhile, whisk the tamari sauce, sugar, tomato paste, Sriracha, vinegar, rosemary, and basil. Cook an additional 5 minutes

Serve garnished with fresh cilantro. Bon appétit!

# Sausage Scallion Balls

*(Ready in about 20 minutes | Servings 4)*
**Per serving:** 560 Calories; 42.2g Fat; 21.5g Carbs; 31.1g Protein; 3.5g Sugars

*Ingredients*

1 ½ pounds beef sausage meat

1 cup rolled oats

4 tablespoons scallions, chopped

1 teaspoon Worcestershire sauce

Flaky sea salt and freshly ground black pepper, to taste

1 teaspoon paprika

1/2 teaspoon granulated garlic

1 teaspoon dried basil

1/2 teaspoon dried oregano

4 teaspoons mustard

4 pickled cucumbers

*Directions*

Start by preheating your Air Fryer to 380 degrees F. Spritz the Air Fryer basket with cooking oil.

In a mixing bowl, thoroughly combine the sausage meat, oats, scallions, Worcestershire sauce, salt, black pepper, paprika, garlic, basil, and oregano.

Then, form the mixture into equal sized meatballs using a tablespoon.

Place the meatballs in the Air Fryer basket and cook for 15 minutes, turning halfway through the cooking time.

Serve with mustard and cucumbers. Bon appétit!

# Cube Steak with Cowboy Sauce

*(Ready in about 20 minutes | Servings 4)*
**Per serving:** 469 Calories; 30.4g Fat; 0.6g Carbs; 46g Protein; 0g Sugars

*Ingredients*

1 ½ pounds cube steak

Salt, to taste

1/4 teaspoon ground black pepper, or more to taste

4 ounces butter

2 garlic cloves, finely chopped

2 scallions, finely chopped

2 tablespoon fresh parsley, finely chopped

1 tablespoon fresh horseradish, grated

1 teaspoon cayenne pepper

*Directions*

Pat dry the cube steak and season it with salt and black pepper. Spritz the Air Fryer basket with cooking oil. Add the meat to the basket.

Cook in the preheated Air Fryer at 400 degrees F for 14 minutes.

Meanwhile, melt the butter in a skillet over a moderate heat. Add the remaining ingredients and simmer until the sauce has thickened and reduced slightly.

Top the warm cube steaks with Cowboy sauce and serve immediately.

## Steak Fingers with Lime Sauce

*(Ready in about 20 minutes + marinating time | Servings 4)*

**Per serving:** 471 Calories; 26.3g Fat; 13.9g Carbs; 42.5g Protein; 4.7g Sugars

*Ingredients*

1 ½ pounds sirloin steak

1/4 cup soy sauce

1/4 cup fresh lime juice

1 teaspoon garlic powder

1 teaspoon shallot powder

1 teaspoon celery seeds

1 teaspoon mustard seeds

Coarse sea salt and ground black pepper, to taste

1 teaspoon red pepper flakes

2 eggs, lightly whisked

1 cup breadcrumbs

1/4 cup parmesan cheese

1 teaspoon paprika

*Directions*

Place the steak, soy sauce, lime juice, garlic powder, shallot powder, celery seeds, mustard seeds, salt, black pepper, and red pepper in a large ceramic bowl; let it marinate for 3 hours.

Tenderize the cube steak by pounding with a mallet; cut into 1-inch strips.

In a shallow bowl, whisk the eggs. In another bowl, mix the breadcrumbs, parmesan cheese, and paprika.

Dip the beef pieces into the whisked eggs and coat on all sides. Now, dredge the beef pieces in the breadcrumb mixture.

Cook at 400 degrees F for 14 minutes, flipping halfway through the cooking time.

Meanwhile, make the sauce by heating the reserved marinade in a saucepan over medium heat; let it simmer until thoroughly warmed. Serve the steak fingers with the sauce on the side. Enjoy!

## Beef Kofta Sandwich

*(Ready in about 30 minutes | Servings 4)*

**Per serving:** 436 Calories; 20.5g Fat; 32g Carbs; 33.7g Protein; 4.1g Sugars

*Ingredients*

1/2 cup leeks, chopped

2 garlic cloves, smashed

1 pound ground chuck

1 slice of bread, soaked in water until fully tender

Salt, to taste

1/4 teaspoon ground black pepper, or more to taste

1 teaspoon cayenne pepper

1/2 teaspoon ground sumac

3 saffron threads

2 tablespoons loosely packed fresh continental parsley leaves

4 tablespoons tahini sauce

4 warm flatbread

4 ounces baby arugula

2 tomatoes, cut into slices

*Directions*

In a bowl, mix the chopped leeks, garlic, ground meat, soaked bread, and spices; knead with your hands until everything is well incorporated.

Now, mound the beef mixture around a wooden skewer into a pointed-ended sausage.

Cook in the preheated Air Fryer at 360 degrees F for 25 minutes.

To make the sandwiches, spread the tahini sauce on the flatbread; top with the kofta kebabs, baby arugula and tomatoes. Enjoy!

# Classic Beef Ribs

*(Ready in about 35 minutes | Servings 4)*

**Per serving:** 532 Calories; 39g Fat; 0.4g Carbs; 44.7g Protein; 0g Sugars

*Ingredients*

2 pounds beef back ribs

1 tablespoon sunflower oil

1/2 teaspoon mixed peppercorns, cracked

1 teaspoon red pepper flakes

1 teaspoon dry mustard

Coarse sea salt, to taste

*Directions*

Trim the excess fat from the beef ribs. Mix the sunflower oil, cracked peppercorns, red pepper, dry mustard, and salt.

Rub over the ribs.

Cook in the preheated Air Fryer at 395 degrees F for 11 minutes

Turn the heat to 330 degrees F and continue to cook for 18 minutes more. Serve warm.

# Spicy Short Ribs with Red Wine Sauce

*(Ready in about 20 minutes + marinating time | Servings 4)*

**Per serving:** 505 Calories; 31g Fat; 22.1g Carbs; 35.2g Protein; 15.3g Sugars

*Ingredients*

1 ½ pounds short ribs

1 cup red wine

1/2 cup tamari sauce

1 lemon, juiced

1 teaspoon fresh ginger, grated

1 teaspoon salt

1 teaspoon black pepper

1 teaspoon paprika

1 teaspoon chipotle chili powder

1 cup ketchup

1 teaspoon garlic powder

1 teaspoon cumin

*Directions*

In a ceramic bowl, place the beef ribs, wine, tamari sauce, lemon juice, ginger, salt, black pepper, paprika, and chipotle chili powder. Cover and let it marinate for 3 hours in the refrigerator.

Discard the marinade and add the short ribs to the Air Fryer basket. Cook in the preheated Air fry at 380 degrees F for 10 minutes, turning them over halfway through the cooking time.

In the meantime, heat the saucepan over medium heat; add the reserved marinade and stir in the ketchup, garlic powder, and cumin. Cook until the sauce has thickened slightly.

Pour the sauce over the warm ribs and serve immediately. Bon appétit!

# Beef Schnitzel with Buttermilk Spaetzle

*(Ready in about 20 minutes | Servings 2)*

**Per serving:** 522 Calories; 20.7g Fat; 17.1g Carbs; 62.2g Protein; 1.8g Sugars

### Ingredients

1 egg, beaten

1/2 teaspoon ground black pepper

1 teaspoon paprika

1/2 teaspoon coarse sea salt

1 tablespoon ghee, melted

1/2 cup tortilla chips, crushed

2 thin-cut minute steaks

Buttermilk Spaetzle:

2 eggs

1/2 cup buttermilk

1/2 cup all-purpose flour

1/2 teaspoon salt

### Directions

Start by preheating your Air Fryer to 360 degrees F.

In a shallow bowl, whisk the egg with black pepper, paprika, and salt.

Thoroughly combine the ghee with the crushed tortilla chips and coarse sea salt in another shallow bowl.

Using a meat mallet, pound the schnitzel to 1/4-inch thick.

Dip the schnitzel into the egg mixture; then, roll the schnitzel over the crumb mixture until coated on all sides.

Cook for 13 minutes in the preheated Air Fryer.

To make the spaetzle, whisk the eggs, buttermilk, flour, and salt in a bowl. Bring a large saucepan of salted water to a boil.

Push the spaetzle mixture through the holes of a potato ricer into the boiling water; slice them off using a table knife. Work in batches.

When the spaetzle float, take them out with a slotted spoon. Repeat with the rest of the spaetzle mixture.

Serve with warm schnitzel. Enjoy!

# Beef Sausage Goulash

*(Ready in about 40 minutes | Servings 2)*

**Per serving:** 565 Calories; 47.1g Fat; 14.3g Carbs; 20.6g Protein; 5.2g Sugars

### Ingredients

1 tablespoon lard, melted

1 shallot, chopped

1 bell pepper, chopped

2 red chilies, finely chopped

1 teaspoon ginger-garlic paste

Sea salt, to taste

1/4 teaspoon ground black pepper

4 beef good quality sausages, thinly sliced

2 teaspoons smoked paprika

1 cup beef bone broth

1/2 cup tomato puree

2 handfuls spring greens, shredded

### Directions

Melt the lard in a Dutch oven over medium-high flame; sauté the shallots and peppers about 4 minutes or until fragrant.

Add the ginger-garlic paste and cook an additional minute. Season with salt and black pepper and transfer to a lightly greased baking pan.

Then, brown the sausages, stirring occasionally, working in batches. Add to the baking pan.

Add the smoked paprika, broth, and tomato puree. Lower the pan onto the Air Fryer basket. Bake at 325 degrees F for 30 minutes.

Stir in the spring greens and cook for 5 minutes more or until they wilt. Serve over the hot rice if desired. Bon appétit!

## Mom's Toad in the Hole

*(Ready in about 45 minutes | Servings 4)*
**Per serving:** 584 Calories; 40.2g Fat; 29.5g Carbs; 23.4g Protein; 3.4g Sugars

*Ingredients*
6 beef sausages
1 tablespoon butter, melted
1 cup plain flour
A pinch of salt
2 eggs
1 cup semi-skimmed milk

*Directions*
Cook the sausages in the preheated Air Fryer at 380 degrees F for 15 minutes, shaking halfway through the cooking time.
Meanwhile, make up the batter mix.
Tip the flour into a bowl with salt; make a well in the middle and crack the eggs into it. Mix with an electric whisk; now, slowly and gradually pour in the milk, whisking all the time.
Place the sausages in a lightly greased baking pan. Pour the prepared batter over the sausages.
Cook in the preheated Air Fryer at 370 degrees F approximately 25 minutes, until golden and risen. Serve with gravy if desired. Bon appétit!

## Beef Nuggets with Cheesy Mushrooms

*(Ready in about 25 minutes | Servings 4)*

**Per serving:** 355 Calories; 15.7g Fat; 13.6g Carbs; 39.8g Protein; 3.4g Sugars

*Ingredients*
2 eggs, beaten
4 tablespoons yogurt
1 cup tortilla chips, crushed
1 teaspoon dry mesquite flavored seasoning mix
Coarse salt and ground black pepper, to taste
1/2 teaspoon onion powder
1 pound cube steak, cut into bite-size pieces
1 pound button mushrooms
1 cup Swiss cheese, shredded

*Directions*
In a shallow bowl, beat the eggs and yogurt. In a resealable bag, mix the tortilla chips, mesquite seasoning, salt, pepper, and onion powder.
Dip the steak pieces in the egg mixture; then, place in the bag, and shake to coat on all sides.
Cook at 400 degrees F for 14 minutes, flipping halfway through the cooking time.
Add the mushrooms to the lightly greased cooking basket. Top with shredded Swiss cheese. Bake in the preheated Air Fryer at 400 degrees F for 5 minutes. Serve with the beef nuggets. Bon appétit!

## Asian-Style Beef Dumplings

*(Ready in about 25 minutes | Servings 5)*
**Per serving:** 353 Calories; 16.7g Fat; 29.5g Carbs; 23.1g Protein; 3.4g Sugars

*Ingredients*
1/2 pound ground chuck
1/2 pound beef sausage, chopped
1 cup Chinese cabbage, shredded
1 bell pepper, chopped
1 onion, chopped
2 garlic cloves, minced
1 medium-sized egg, beaten

Sea salt and ground black pepper, to taste

20 wonton wrappers

2 tablespoons soy sauce

2 teaspoons sesame oil

2 teaspoons sesame seeds, lightly toasted

2 tablespoons seasoned rice vinegar

1/2 teaspoon chili sauce

### Directions

To make the filling, thoroughly combine the ground chuck, sausage, cabbage, bell pepper, onion, garlic, egg, salt, and black pepper.

Place the wrappers on a clean and dry surface. Now, divide the filling among the wrappers.

Then, fold each dumpling in half and pinch to seal.

Transfer the dumplings to the lightly greased cooking basket. Bake at 390 degrees F for 15 minutes, turning over halfway through.

In the meantime, mix the soy sauce, sesame oil, sesame seeds, rice vinegar, and chili sauce. Serve the beef dumplings with the sauce on the side. Enjoy!

# FISH & SEAFOOD

## Monkfish Fillets with Romano Cheese

*(Ready in about 15 minutes | Servings 2)*
**Per serving:** 415 Calories; 22.5g Fat; 3.7g Carbs; 47.4g Protein; 2.3g Sugars

*Ingredients*
2 monkfish fillets
1 teaspoon garlic paste
2 tablespoons butter, melted
1/2 teaspoon Aleppo chili powder
1/2 teaspoon dried rosemary
1/4 teaspoon cracked black pepper
1/2 teaspoon sea salt
4 tablespoons Romano cheese, grated

*Directions*
Start by preheating the Air Fryer to 320 degrees F. Spritz the Air Fryer basket with cooking oil. Spread the garlic paste all over the fish fillets.
Brush the monkfish fillets with the melted butter on both sides. Sprinkle with the chili powder, rosemary, black pepper, and salt. Cook for 7 minutes in the preheated Air Fryer.
Top with the Romano cheese and continue to cook for 2 minutes more or until heated through. Bon appétit!

## Grilled Hake with Garlic Sauce

*(Ready in about 20 minutes | Servings 3)*
**Per serving:** 479 Calories; 22g Fat; 29.1g Carbs; 39.1g Protein; 3.6g Sugars

*Ingredients*
3 hake fillets
6 tablespoons mayonnaise
1 teaspoon Dijon mustard
1 tablespoon fresh lime juice
1 cup panko crumbs
Salt, to taste
1/4 teaspoon ground black pepper, or more to taste
Garlic Sauce
1/4 cup Greek-style yogurt
2 tablespoons olive oil
2 cloves garlic, minced
1/2 teaspoon tarragon leaves, minced

*Directions*
Pat dry the hake fillets with a kitchen towel.
In a shallow bowl, whisk together the mayo, mustard, and lime juice. In another shallow bowl, thoroughly combine the panko crumbs with salt, and black pepper.
Spritz the Air Fryer grill pan with non-stick cooking spray. Grill in the preheated Air Fry at 395 degrees F for 10 minutes, flipping halfway through the cooking time.
Serve immediately.

## Grilled Tilapia with Portobello Mushrooms

*(Ready in about 20 minutes | Servings 2)*
**Per serving:** 320 Calories; 11.4g Fat; 29.1g Carbs; 49.3g Protein; 4.2g Sugars

*Ingredients*
2 tilapia fillets
1 tablespoon avocado oil
1/2 teaspoon red pepper flakes, crushed
1/2 teaspoon dried sage, crushed
1/4 teaspoon lemon pepper
1/2 teaspoon sea salt
1 teaspoon dried parsley flakes

4 medium-sized Portobello mushrooms

A few drizzles of liquid smoke

**Directions**

Toss all ingredients in a mixing bowl; except for the mushrooms.

Transfer the tilapia fillets to a lightly greased grill pan. Preheat your Air Fryer to 400 degrees F and cook the tilapia fillets for 5 minutes.

Now, turn the fillets over and add the Portobello mushrooms. Continue to cook for 5 minutes longer or until mushrooms are tender and the fish is opaque. Serve immediately.

## Authentic Mediterranean Calamari Salad

*(Ready in about 15 minutes | Servings 3)*

**Per serving:** 457 Calories; 31.3g Fat; 18.4g Carbs; 25.1g Protein; 9.2g Sugars

1 pound squid, cleaned, sliced into rings

2 tablespoons sherry wine

1/2 teaspoon granulated garlic

Salt, to taste

1/2 teaspoon ground black pepper

1/2 teaspoon basil

1/2 teaspoon dried rosemary

1 cup grape tomatoes

1 small red onion, thinly sliced

1/3 cup Kalamata olives, pitted and sliced

1/2 cup mayonnaise

1 teaspoon yellow mustard

1/2 cup fresh flat-leaf parsley leaves, coarsely chopped

**Directions**

Start by preheating the Air Fryer to 400 degrees F. Spritz the Air Fryer basket with cooking oil.

Toss the squid rings with the sherry wine, garlic, salt, pepper, basil, and rosemary. Cook in the preheated Air Fryer for 5 minutes, shaking the basket halfway through the cooking time.

Work in batches and let it cool to room temperature. When the squid is cool enough, add the remaining ingredients.

Gently stir to combine and serve well chilled. Bon appétit!

## Shrimp Scampi Linguine

*(Ready in about 25 minutes | Servings 4)*

**Per serving:** 560 Calories; 15.1g Fat; 47.3g Carbs; 59.3g Protein; 1.6g Sugars

1 ½ pounds shrimp, shelled and deveined

1/2 tablespoon fresh basil leaves, chopped

2 tablespoons olive oil

2 cloves garlic, minced

1/2 teaspoon fresh ginger, grated

1/4 teaspoon cracked black pepper

1/2 teaspoon sea salt

1/4 cup chicken stock

2 ripe tomatoes, pureed

8 ounces linguine pasta

1/2 cup parmesan cheese, preferably freshly grated

**Directions**

Start by preheating the Air Fryer to 395 degrees F. Place the shrimp, basil, olive oil, garlic, ginger, black pepper, salt, chicken stock, and tomatoes in the casserole dish.

Transfer the casserole dish to the cooking basket and bake for 10 minutes.

Bring a large pot of lightly salted water to a boil. Cook the linguine for 10 minutes or until al dente; drain.

Divide between four serving plates. Add the shrimp sauce and top with parmesan cheese. Bon appétit!

# Sunday Fish with Sticky Sauce

*(Ready in about 20 minutes | Servings 2)*

**Per serving:** 573 Calories; 38.3g Fat; 31.5g Carbs; 26.2g Protein; 5.7g Sugars

*Ingredients*

2 pollack fillets

Salt and black pepper, to taste

1 tablespoon olive oil

1 cup chicken broth

2 tablespoons light soy sauce

1 tablespoon brown sugar

2 tablespoons butter, melted

1 teaspoon fresh ginger, minced

1 teaspoon fresh garlic, minced

2 corn tortillas

*Directions*

Pat dry the pollack fillets and season them with salt and black pepper; drizzle the sesame oil all over the fish fillets.

Preheat the Air Fryer to 380 degrees F and cook your fish for 11 minutes. Slice into bite-sized pieces.

Meanwhile, prepare the sauce. Add the broth to a large saucepan and bring to a boil. Add the soy sauce, sugar, butter, ginger, and garlic. Reduce the heat to simmer and cook until it is reduced slightly.

Add the fish pieces to the warm sauce. Serve on corn tortillas and enjoy!

# Buttermilk Tuna fillets

*(Ready in about 50 minutes | Servings 3)*

**Per serving:** 266 Calories; 5.7g Fat; 13.6g Carbs; 37.8g Protein; 2.5g Sugars

*Ingredients*

1 pound tuna fillets

1/2 cup buttermilk

1/2 cup tortilla chips, crushed

1/4 cup parmesan cheese, grated

1/4 cup cassava flour

Salt and ground black pepper, to taste

1 teaspoon mustard seeds

1 teaspoon paprika

1 teaspoon garlic powder

1/2 teaspoon onion powder

*Directions*

Place the tuna fillets and buttermilk in a bowl; cover and let it sit for 30 minutes.

In a shallow bowl, thoroughly combine the remaining ingredients; mix until well combined.

Dip the tuna fillets in the parmesan mixture until they are covered on all sides.

Cook in the preheated Air Fryer at 380 degrees F for 12 minutes, turning halfway through the cooking time. Bon appétit!

# Swordfish with Roasted Peppers and Garlic Sauce

*(Ready in about 30 minutes | Servings 3)*

**Per serving:** 274 Calories; 14.1g Fat; 5.1g Carbs; 30.5g Protein; 3.2g Sugars

*Ingredients*

3 bell peppers

3 swordfish steaks

1 tablespoon butter, melted

2 garlic cloves, minced

Sea salt and freshly ground black pepper, to taste

1/2 teaspoon cayenne pepper

1/2 teaspoon ginger powder

*Directions*

Start by preheating your Air Fryer to 400 degrees F. Brush the Air Fryer basket lightly with cooking oil.

Then, roast the bell peppers for 5 minutes. Give the peppers a half turn; place them back in the cooking basket and roast for another 5 minutes. Turn them one more time and roast until the skin is charred and soft or 5 more minutes. Peel the peppers and set aside.

Then, add the swordfish steaks to the lightly greased cooking basket and cook at 400 degrees F for 10 minutes.

Meanwhile, melt the butter in a small saucepan. Cook the garlic until fragrant and add the salt, pepper, cayenne pepper, and ginger powder. Cook until everything is thoroughly heated.

Plate the peeled peppers and the roasted swordfish; spoon the sauce over them and serve warm.

## Shrimp Scampi Dip with Cheese

*(Ready in about 25 minutes | Servings 8)*
**Per serving:** 135 Calories; 9.7g Fat; 3.3g Carbs; 8.7g Protein; 1g Sugars

*Ingredients*

2 teaspoons butter, melted
8 ounces shrimp, peeled and deveined
2 garlic cloves, minced
1/4 cup chicken stock
2 tablespoons fresh lemon juice
Salt and ground black pepper, to taste
1/2 teaspoon red pepper flakes
4 ounces cream cheese, at room temperature
1/2 cup sour cream
4 tablespoons mayonnaise
1/4 cup mozzarella cheese, shredded

*Directions*

Start by preheating the Air Fryer to 395 degrees F. Grease the sides and bottom of a baking dish with the melted butter.

Place the shrimp, garlic, chicken stock, lemon juice, salt, black pepper, and red pepper flakes in the baking dish.

Transfer the baking dish to the cooking basket and bake for 10 minutes. Add the mixture to your food processor; pulse until the coarsely is chopped.

Add the cream cheese, sour cream, and mayonnaise. Top with the mozzarella cheese and bake in the preheated Air Fryer at 360 degrees F for 6 to 7 minutes or until the cheese is bubbling. Serve immediately with breadsticks if desired. Bon appétit!

## Filet of Flounder Cutlets

*(Ready in about 15 minutes | Servings 2)*
**Per serving:** 330 Calories; 20.3g Fat; 12.1g Carbs; 24.8g Protein; 2.3g Sugars

*Ingredients*

1 egg
1/2 cup cracker crumbs
1/2 cup Pecorino Romano cheese, grated
Sea salt and white pepper, to taste
1/2 teaspoon cayenne pepper
1 teaspoon dried parsley flakes
2 flounder fillets

*Directions*

To make a breading station, whisk the egg until frothy.

In another bowl, mix the cracker crumbs, Pecorino Romano cheese, and spices.

Dip the fish in the egg mixture and turn to coat evenly; then, dredge in the cracker crumb mixture, turning a couple of times to coat evenly.

Cook in the preheated Air Fryer at 390 degrees F for 5 minutes; turn them over and cook another 5 minutes. Enjoy!

# King Prawns with Lemon Butter Sauce

*(Ready in about 15 minutes | Servings 4)*
**Per serving:** 302 Calories; 17.2g Fat; 3.2g Carbs; 32.2g Protein; 0.2g Sugars

*Ingredients*
King Prawns:
1 ½ pounds king prawns, peeled and deveined
2 cloves garlic, minced
1/2 cup Pecorino Romano cheese, grated
Sea salt and ground white pepper, to your liking
1/2 teaspoon onion powder
1 teaspoon garlic powder
1 teaspoon mustard seeds
2 tablespoons olive oil
Sauce:
2 tablespoons butter
2 tablespoons fresh lemon juice
1/2 teaspoon Worcestershire sauce
1/4 teaspoon ground black pepper

*Directions*
In a plastic closeable bag, thoroughly combine all ingredients for the king prawns; shake to combine well.

Transfer the coated king prawns to the lightly greased Air Fryer basket.

Cook in the preheated Air Fryer at 390 degrees for 6 minutes, shaking the basket halfway through. Work in batches.

In the meantime, heat a small saucepan over a moderate flame; melt the butter and add the remaining ingredients.

Turn the temperature to low and whisk for 2 to 3 minutes until thoroughly heated. Spoon the sauce onto the warm king prawns. Bon appétit!

# Crusty Catfish with Sweet Potato Fries

*(Ready in about 50 minutes | Servings 2)*
**Per serving:** 481 Calories; 25.4g Fat; 37.5g Carbs; 31.3g Protein; 6.6g Sugars

*Ingredients*
1/2 pound catfish
1/2 cup bran cereal
1/4 cup parmesan cheese, grated
Sea salt and ground black pepper, to taste
1 teaspoon smoked paprika
1 teaspoon garlic powder
1/4 teaspoon ground bay leaf
1 egg
2 tablespoons butter, melted
4 sweet potatoes, cut French fries

*Directions*
Pat the catfish dry with a kitchen towel.

Combine the bran cereal with the parmesan cheese and all spices in a shallow bowl. Whisk the egg in another shallow bowl.

Dip the fish in the egg mixture and turn to coat evenly; then, dredge in the bran cereal mixture, turning a couple of times to coat evenly.

Spritz the Air Fryer basket with cooking spray. Cook the catfish in the preheated Air Fryer at 390 degrees F for 10 minutes; turn them over and cook for 4 minutes more.

Then, drizzle the melted butter all over the sweet potatoes; cook them in the preheated Air Fryer at 380 degrees F for 30 minutes, shaking occasionally. Serve over the warm fish fillets. Bon appétit!

# Crunchy Topped Fish Bake

*(Ready in about 20 minutes | Servings 4)*
**Per serving:** 455 Calories; 12.4g Fat; 9.9g Carbs; 73.6g Protein; 3.1g Sugars

*Ingredients*

1 tablespoon butter, melted

1 medium-sized leek, thinly sliced

1 tablespoon chicken stock

1 tablespoon dry white wine

1 pound tuna

1/2 teaspoon red pepper flakes, crushed

Sea salt and ground black pepper, to taste

1/2 teaspoon dried rosemary

1/2 teaspoon dried basil

1/2 teaspoon dried thyme

2 ripe tomatoes, pureed

1/4 cup breadcrumbs

1/4 cup Parmesan cheese, grated

*Directions*

Melt 1/2 tablespoon of butter in a sauté pan over medium-high heat. Now, cook the leek and garlic until tender and aromatic. Add the stock and wine to deglaze the pan.

Preheat your Air Fryer to 370 degrees F.

Grease a casserole dish with the remaining 1/2 tablespoon of melted butter. Place the fish in the casserole dish. Add the seasonings. Top with the sautéed leek mixture.

Add the tomato puree. Cook for 10 minutes in the preheated Air Fryer. Top with the breadcrumbs and cheese; cook an additional 7 minutes until the crumbs are golden. Bon appétit!

# Creamed Trout Salad

*(Ready in about 20 minutes | Servings 2)*
**Per serving:** 490 Calories; 26.4g Fat; 30.3g Carbs; 33.9g Protein; 7.8g Sugars

*Ingredients*

1/2 pound trout fillets, skinless

2 tablespoons horseradish, prepared, drained

1/4 cup mayonnaise

1 tablespoon fresh lemon juice

1 teaspoon mustard

Salt and ground white pepper, to taste

6 ounces chickpeas, canned and drained

1 red onion, thinly sliced

1 cup Iceberg lettuce, torn into pieces

*Directions*

Spritz the Air Fryer basket with cooking spray.

Cook the trout fillets in the preheated Air Fryer at 395 degrees F for 10 minutes or until opaque. Make sure to turn them halfway through the cooking time.

Break the fish into bite-sized chunks and place in the refrigerator to cool. Toss your fish with the remaining ingredients. Bon appétit!

# Roasted Mediterranean Snapper Fillets

*(Ready in about 20 minutes + marinating time | Servings 3)*
**Per serving:** 271 Calories; 4.6g Fat; 21.8g Carbs; 34.9g Protein; 4.9g Sugars

*Ingredients*

Marinade:

1 tablespoon black olives, chopped

1/4 cup dry white wine

2 tablespoons fresh lemon juice

1/2 teaspoon dried oregano

1/2 teaspoon dried basil

1 tablespoon parsley leaves, chopped

1 tomato, pureed

Roasted Snapper:

1 pound snapper fillets

1/2 cup cassava flour

Salt and white pepper, to taste

*Directions*

Add all ingredients for the marinade to a large ceramic bowl. Add the snapper fillets and let them marinate for 1 hour in your refrigerator.

Place the cassava flour on a tray; now, coat the snapper fillets with the cassava flour. Season with salt and pepper.

Cook the snapper fillets in the preheated Air Fryer at 395 degrees F for 10 minutes, basting with the marinade and flipping them halfway through the cooking time. Bon appétit!

## Orange Glazed Scallops

*(Ready in about 15 minutes | Servings 3)*

**Per serving:** 229 Calories; 6.7g Fat; 10.9g Carbs; 31.5g Protein; 2.1g Sugars

*Ingredients*

1 pound jumbo sea scallops

1 tablespoon soy sauce

2 tablespoons orange juice

1 teaspoon orange zest

1/2 teaspoon fresh parsley, minced

1 tablespoon olive oil

Sea salt, to taste

1/2 teaspoon ground black pepper

*Directions*

Start by preheating your Air Fryer to 400 degrees F.

Toss all ingredients in mixing bowl.

Place the scallops in the lightly greased cooking basket and cook for 7 minutes, shaking the basket halfway through the cooking time. Work in batches.

Taste, adjust the seasonings and serve warm. Bon appétit!

## Beer Battered Fish with Honey Tartar Sauce

*(Ready in about 20 minutes | Servings 2)*

**Per serving:** 424 Calories; 9.7g Fat; 36.5g Carbs; 34.1g Protein; 4.1g Sugars

*Ingredients*

1/2 pound hoki fillets

Sea salt and black pepper, to taste

1/2 cup flour

1 egg

1 teaspoon paprika

1 (12-ounce) bottle beer

1/4 cup mayonnaise

1/2 teaspoon honey

1 tablespoon fresh lemon juice

1 teaspoon Dijon mustard

1 teaspoon sweet pickle relish

*Directions*

Rinse the hoki fillets and pat dry.

Combine the flour, egg and paprika in a bowl. Gradually pour in beer until a batter is formed.

Dip the fish fillets into the batter; then, transfer to the lightly greased cooking basket. Cook in the preheated Air Fryer at 380 degrees F for 12 minutes.

In the meantime, whisk the remaining ingredients to make the sauce. Place in the refrigerator until ready to serve. Bon appétit!

## Halibut with Thai Lemongrass Marinade

*(Ready in about 45 minutes | Servings 2)*

**Per serving:** 359 Calories; 16.7g Fat; 7.8g Carbs; 43.4g Protein; 2.9g Sugars

*Ingredients*

2 tablespoons tamari sauce

2 tablespoons fresh lime juice

2 tablespoons olive oil

1 teaspoon Thai curry paste

1/2 inch lemongrass, finely chopped

1 teaspoon basil

2 cloves garlic, minced

2 tablespoons shallot, minced

Sea salt and ground black pepper, to taste

2 halibut steaks

### Directions

Place all ingredients in a ceramic dish; let it marinate for 30 minutes.

Place the halibut steaks in the lightly greased cooking basket.

Bake in the preheated Air Fryer at 400 degrees F for 9 to 10 minutes, basting with the reserved marinade and flipping them halfway through the cooking time. Bon appétit!

## Sea Bass with French Sauce Tartare

*(Ready in about 15 minutes | Servings 2)*

**Per serving:** 384 Calories; 28.5g Fat; 3.5g Carbs; 27.6g Protein; 1g Sugars

### Ingredients

1 tablespoon olive oil

2 sea bass fillets

Sauce:

1/2 cup mayonnaise

1 tablespoon capers, drained and chopped

1 tablespoon gherkins, drained and chopped

2 tablespoons scallions, finely chopped

2 tablespoons lemon juice

### Directions

Start by preheating your Air Fryer to 395 degrees F. Drizzle olive oil all over the fish fillets.

Cook the sea bass in the preheated Air Fryer for 10 minutes, flipping them halfway through the cooking time.

Meanwhile, make the sauce by whisking the remaining ingredients until everything is well incorporated. Place in the refrigerator until ready to serve. Bon appétit!

## Jamaican-Style Fish and Potato Fritters

*(Ready in about 30 minutes | Servings 2)*

**Per serving:** 322 Calories; 14g Fat; 27.4g Carbs; 22.1g Protein; 4.2g Sugars

### Ingredients

1/2 pound sole fillets

1/2 pound mashed potatoes

1 egg, well beaten

1/2 cup red onion, chopped

2 garlic cloves, minced

2 tablespoons fresh parsley, chopped

1 bell pepper, finely chopped

1/2 teaspoon scotch bonnet pepper, minced

1 tablespoon olive oil

1 tablespoon coconut aminos

1/2 teaspoon paprika

Salt and white pepper, to taste

### Directions

Start by preheating your Air Fryer to 395 degrees F. Spritz the sides and bottom of the cooking basket with cooking spray.

Cook the sole fillets in the preheated Air Fryer for 10 minutes, flipping them halfway through the cooking time.

In a mixing bowl, mash the sole fillets into flakes. Stir in the remaining ingredients. Shape the fish mixture into patties.

Bake in the preheated Air Fryer at 390 degrees F for 14 minutes, flipping them halfway through the cooking time. Bon appétit!

# Quick Thai Coconut Fish

*(Ready in about 20 minutes + marinating time | Servings 2)*

**Per serving:** 435 Calories; 21.5g Fat; 11.6g Carbs; 50.2g Protein; 8.7g Sugars

*Ingredients*

1 cup coconut milk

2 tablespoons lime juice

2 tablespoons Shoyu sauce

Salt and white pepper, to taste

1 teaspoon turmeric powder

1/2 teaspoon ginger powder

1/2 Thai Bird's Eye chili, seeded and finely chopped

1 pound tilapia

2 tablespoons olive oil

*Directions*

In a mixing bowl, thoroughly combine the coconut milk with the lime juice, Shoyu sauce, salt, pepper, turmeric, ginger, and chili pepper. Add tilapia and let it marinate for 1 hour.

Brush the Air Fryer basket with olive oil. Discard the marinade and place the tilapia fillets in the Air Fryer basket.

Cook the tilapia in the preheated Air Fryer at 400 degrees F for 6 minutes; turn them over and cook for 6 minutes more. Work in batches.

Serve with some extra lime wedges if desired. Enjoy!

# Double Cheese Fish Casserole

*(Ready in about 30 minutes | Servings 4)*

**Per serving:** 456 Calories; 30.1g Fat; 8.8g Carbs; 36.7g Protein; 3g Sugars

*Ingredients*

1 tablespoon avocado oil

1 pound hake fillets

1 teaspoon garlic powder

Sea salt and ground white pepper, to taste

2 tablespoons shallots, chopped

1 bell pepper, seeded and chopped

1/2 cup Cottage cheese

1/2 cup sour cream

1 egg, well whisked

1 teaspoon yellow mustard

1 tablespoon lime juice

1/2 cup Swiss cheese, shredded

*Directions*

Brush the bottom and sides of a casserole dish with avocado oil. Add the hake fillets to the casserole dish and sprinkle with garlic powder, salt, and pepper.

Add the chopped shallots and bell peppers.

In a mixing bowl, thoroughly combine the Cottage cheese, sour cream, egg, mustard, and lime juice. Pour the mixture over fish and spread evenly.

Cook in the preheated Air Fryer at 370 degrees F for 10 minutes.

Top with the Swiss cheese and cook an additional 7 minutes. Let it rest for 10 minutes before slicing and serving. Bon appétit!

# Rosemary-Infused Butter Scallops

*(Ready in about 1 hour 10 minutes | Servings 4)*

**Per serving:** 317 Calories; 17.3g Fat; 9.2g Carbs; 29.4g Protein; 0.2g Sugars

*Ingredients*

2 pounds sea scallops

1/2 cup beer

4 tablespoons butter

2 sprigs rosemary, only leaves

Sea salt and freshly cracked black pepper, to taste

### Directions

In a ceramic dish, mix the sea scallops with beer; let it marinate for 1 hour.

Meanwhile, preheat your Air Fryer to 400 degrees F. Melt the butter and add the rosemary leaves. Stir for a few minutes.

Discard the marinade and transfer the sea scallops to the Air Fryer basket. Season with salt and black pepper.

Cook the scallops in the preheated Air Fryer for 7 minutes, shaking the basket halfway through the cooking time. Work in batches.

Bon appétit!

## Shrimp Kabobs with Cherry Tomatoes

*(Ready in about 30 minutes | Servings 4)*

**Per serving:** 267 Calories; 6.8g Fat; 18.1g Carbs; 35.4g Protein; 14.5g Sugars

### Ingredients

1 ½ pounds jumbo shrimp, cleaned, shelled and deveined

1 pound cherry tomatoes

2 tablespoons butter, melted

1 tablespoons Sriracha sauce

Sea salt and ground black pepper, to taste

1/2 teaspoon dried oregano

1/2 teaspoon dried basil

1 teaspoon dried parsley flakes

1/2 teaspoon marjoram

1/2 teaspoon mustard seeds

### Directions

Toss all ingredients in a mixing bowl until the shrimp and tomatoes are covered on all sides.

Soak the wooden skewers in water for 15 minutes. Thread the jumbo shrimp and cherry tomatoes onto skewers. Cook in the preheated Air Fryer at 400 degrees F for 5 minutes, working with batches. Bon appétit!

## Snapper with Coconut Milk Sauce

*(Ready in about 20 minutes + marinating time | Servings 2)*

**Per serving:** 431 Calories; 17.3g Fat; 18.5g Carbs; 48.4g Protein; 0.4g Sugars

### Ingredients

1/2 cup full-fat coconut milk

2 tablespoons lemon juice

1 teaspoon fresh ginger, grated

2 snapper fillets

1 tablespoon olive oil

1 tablespoon cornstarch

Salt and white pepper, to taste

### Directions

Place the milk, lemon juice, and ginger in a glass bowl; add fish and let it marinate for 1 hour.

Removed the fish from the milk mixture and place in the Air Fryer basket. Drizzle olive oil all over the fish fillets.

Cook in the preheated Air Fryer at 390 degrees F for 15 minutes.

Meanwhile, heat the milk mixture over medium-high heat; bring to a rapid boil, stirring continuously. Reduce to simmer and add the cornstarch, salt, and pepper; continue to cook 12 minutes more.

Spoon the sauce over the warm snapper fillets and serve immediately. Bon appétit!

## Italian-Style Crab Bruschetta

*(Ready in about 15 minutes | Servings 2)*

**Per serving:** 458 Calories; 32.6g Fat; 15.4g Carbs; 25g Protein; 3.3g Sugars

*Ingredients*

4 slices sourdough bread

2 tablespoons tomato ketchup

4 tablespoons mayonnaise

1 teaspoon fresh rosemary, chopped

8 ounces lump crabmeat

1 teaspoon granulated garlic

2 tablespoons shallots, chopped

4 tablespoons mozzarella cheese, crumbled

*Directions*

Place the slices of sourdough bread on a flat surface.

In a mixing bowl, thoroughly combine the tomato ketchup, mayo, rosemary, crabmeat, garlic, and shallots.

Divide the crabmeat mixture between the slices of bread. Top with mozzarella cheese.

Bake in the preheated Air Fryer at 370 degrees F for 10 minutes. Bon appétit!

## Easy Creamy Shrimp Nachos

*(Ready in about 15 minutes | Servings 4)*

**Per serving:** 535 Calories; 26.9g Fat; 40g Carbs; 34.7g Protein; 1.5g Sugars

*Ingredients*

1 pound shrimp, cleaned and deveined

1 tablespoon olive oil

2 tablespoons fresh lemon juice

1 teaspoon paprika

1/4 teaspoon cumin powder

1/2 teaspoon shallot powder

1/2 teaspoon garlic powder

Coarse sea salt and ground black pepper, to taste

1 (9-ounce) bag corn tortilla chips

1/4 cup pickled jalapeño, minced

1 cup Pepper Jack cheese, grated

1/2 cup sour cream

*Directions*

Toss the shrimp with the olive oil, lemon juice, paprika, cumin powder, shallot powder, garlic powder, salt, and black pepper.

Cook in the preheated Air Fryer at 390 degrees F for 5 minutes.

Place the tortilla chips on the aluminum foil-lined cooking basket. Top with the shrimp mixture, jalapeño and cheese. Cook another 2 minutes or until cheese has melted.

Serve garnished with sour cream and enjoy!

## Tuna Cake Burgers with Beer Cheese Sauce

*(Ready in about 2 hours 20 minutes | Servings 4)*

**Per serving:** 450 Calories; 22.3g Fat; 28.3g Carbs; 33.6g Protein; 3.8g Sugars

*Ingredients*

1 pound canned tuna, drained

1 egg, whisked

1 garlic clove, minced

2 tablespoons shallots, minced

1 cup fresh breadcrumbs

Sea salt and ground black pepper, to taste

1 tablespoon sesame oil

Beer Cheese Sauce:

1 tablespoon butter

1 cup beer

1 tablespoon rice flour

2 tablespoons Colby cheese, grated

### Directions

In a mixing bowl, thoroughly combine the tuna, egg, garlic, shallots, breadcrumbs, salt, and black pepper. Shape the tuna mixture into four patties and place in your refrigerator for 2 hours.

Brush the patties with sesame oil on both sides. Cook in the preheated Air Fryer at 360 degrees F for 14 minutes.

In the meantime, melt the butter in a pan over a moderate heat. Add the beer and flour and whisk until it starts bubbling.

Now, stir in the grated cheese and cook for 3 to 4 minutes longer or until the cheese has melted. Spoon the sauce over the fish cake burgers and serve immediately.

# VEGETABLES & SIDE DISHES

## Winter Vegetable Braise

*(Ready in about 25 minutes | Servings 2)*

**Per serving:** 358 Calories; 12.3g Fat; 55.7g Carbs; 7.7g Protein; 7.4g Sugars

*Ingredients*

4 potatoes, peeled and cut into 1-inch pieces

1 celery root, peeled and cut into 1-inch pieces

1 cup winter squash

2 tablespoons unsalted butter, melted

1/2 cup chicken broth

1/4 cup tomato sauce

1 teaspoon parsley

1 teaspoon rosemary

1 teaspoon thyme

*Directions*

Start by preheating your Air Fryer to 370 degrees F. Add all ingredients in a lightly greased casserole dish. Stir to combine well.

Bake in the preheated Air Fryer for 10 minutes. Gently stir the vegetables with a large spoon and increase temperature to 400 degrees F; cook for 10 minutes more.

Serve in individual bowls with a few drizzles of lemon juice. Bon appétit!

## Family Vegetable Gratin

*(Ready in about 35 minutes | Servings 4)*

**Per serving:** 373 Calories; 26.1g Fat; 17.7g Carbs; 18.7g Protein; 7.7g Sugars

*Ingredients*

1 pound Chinese cabbage, roughly chopped

2 bell peppers, seeded and sliced

1 jalapeno pepper, seeded and sliced

1 onion, thickly sliced

2 garlic cloves, sliced

1/2 stick butter

4 tablespoons all-purpose flour

1 cup milk

1 cup cream cheese

Sea salt and freshly ground black pepper, to taste

1/2 teaspoon cayenne pepper

1 cup Monterey Jack cheese, shredded

*Directions*

Heat a pan of salted water and bring to a boil. Boil the Chinese cabbage for 2 to 3 minutes. Transfer the Chinese cabbage to cold water to stop the cooking process.

Place the Chinese cabbage in a lightly greased casserole dish. Add the peppers, onion, and garlic. Next, melt the butter in a saucepan over a moderate heat. Gradually add the flour and cook for 2 minutes to form a paste.

Slowly pour in the milk, stirring continuously until a thick sauce forms. Add the cream cheese. Season with the salt, black pepper, and cayenne pepper. Add the mixture to the casserole dish.

Top with the shredded Monterey Jack cheese and bake in the preheated Air Fryer at 390 degrees F for 25 minutes. Serve hot.

## Roasted Beet Salad

*(Ready in about 20 minutes + chilling time | Servings 2)*

**Per serving:** 149 Calories; 6.5g Fat; 20.6g Carbs; 3.5g Protein; 13.9g Sugars

*Ingredients*

2 medium-sized beets, peeled and cut into wedges

2 tablespoons extra virgin olive oil

1 tablespoon balsamic vinegar

1 teaspoon yellow mustard

1 garlic clove, minced

1/4 teaspoon cumin powder

Coarse sea salt and ground black pepper, to taste

1 tablespoon fresh parsley leaves, roughly chopped

### Directions

Place the beets in a single layer in the lightly greased cooking basket.

Cook at 370 degrees F for 13 minutes, shaking the basket halfway through the cooking time.

Let it cool to room temperature; toss the beets with the remaining ingredients. Serve well chilled. Enjoy!

# Spicy Ricotta Stuffed Mushrooms

*(Ready in about 35 minutes | Servings 4)*

**Per serving:** 214 Calories; 5.6g Fat; 30.4g Carbs; 12.3g Protein; 5g Sugars

### Ingredients

1/2 pound small white mushrooms

Sea salt and ground black pepper, to taste

2 tablespoons Ricotta cheese

1/2 teaspoon ancho chili powder

1 teaspoon paprika

4 tablespoons all-purpose flour

1 egg

1/2 cup fresh breadcrumbs

### Directions

Remove the stems from the mushroom caps and chop them; mix the chopped mushrooms steams with the salt, black pepper, cheese, chili powder, and paprika.

Stuff the mushroom caps with the cheese filling.

Place the flour in a shallow bowl, and beat the egg in another bowl. Place the breadcrumbs in a third shallow bowl.

Dip the mushrooms in the flour, then, dip in the egg mixture; finally, dredge in the breadcrumbs and press to adhere. Spritz the stuffed mushrooms with cooking spray.

Cook in the preheated Air Fryer at 360 degrees F for 18 minutes. Bon appétit!

# Baked Cholula Cauliflower

*(Ready in about 20 minutes | Servings 4)*

**Per serving:** 153 Calories; 7.3g Fat; 19.3g Carbs; 4.1g Protein; 2.9g Sugars

### Ingredients

1/2 cup all-purpose flour

1/2 cup water

Salt, to taste

1/2 teaspoon ground black pepper

1/2 teaspoon shallot powder

1/2 teaspoon garlic powder

1/2 teaspoon cayenne pepper

2 tablespoons olive oil

1 pound cauliflower, broken into small florets

1/4 cup Cholula sauce

### Directions

Start by preheating your Air Fryer to 400 degrees F. Lightly grease a baking pan with cooking spray. In a mixing bowl, combine the flour, water, spices, and olive oil. Coat the cauliflower with the prepared batter; arrange the cauliflower on the baking pan.

Then, bake in the preheated Air Fryer for 8 minutes or until golden brown.

Brush the Cholula sauce all over the cauliflower florets and bake an additional 4 to 5 minutes. Bon appétit!

# Fall Vegetables with Spiced Yogurt

*(Ready in about 25 minutes | Servings 2)*
**Per serving:** 319 Calories; 14.1g Fat; 46g Carbs; 6.4g Protein; 20.1g Sugars

*Ingredients*
1 pound celeriac, cut into 1 1/2-inch pieces
2 carrots, cut into 1 1/2-inch pieces
2 red onions, cut into 1 1/2-inch pieces
1 tablespoon sesame oil
1/2 teaspoon ground black pepper, to taste
1/2 teaspoon sea salt
Spiced Yogurt:
1/4 cup Greek yogurt
1 tablespoon mayonnaise
1 tablespoon honey
1/2 teaspoon mustard seeds
1/2 teaspoon chili powder

*Directions*
Place the vegetables in a single layer in the lightly greased cooking basket. Drizzle the sesame oil over vegetables.
Sprinkle with black pepper and sea salt.
Cook at 390 degrees F for 20 minutes, shaking the basket halfway through the cooking time.
Meanwhile, make the sauce by whisking all ingredients. Spoon the sauce over the roasted vegetables. Bon appétit!

# Sweet-and-Sour Mixed Veggies

*(Ready in about 25 minutes | Servings 4)*
**Per serving:** 153 Calories; 7.1g Fat; 21.6g Carbs; 3.6g Protein; 14.2g Sugars

*Ingredients*
1/2 pound asparagus, cut into 1 1/2-inch pieces
1/2 pound broccoli, cut into 1 1/2-inch pieces
1/2 pound carrots, cut into 1 1/2-inch pieces
2 tablespoons peanut oil
Some salt and white pepper, to taste
1/2 cup water
4 tablespoons raisins
2 tablespoon honey
2 tablespoons apple cider vinegar

*Directions*
Place the vegetables in a single layer in the lightly greased cooking basket. Drizzle the peanut oil over the vegetables.
Sprinkle with salt and white pepper.
Cook at 380 degrees F for 15 minutes, shaking the basket halfway through the cooking time.
Add 1/2 cup of water to a saucepan; bring to a rapid boil and add the raisins, honey, and vinegar.
Cook for 5 to 7 minutes or until the sauce has reduced by half.
Spoon the sauce over the warm vegetables and serve immediately. Bon appétit!

# Roasted Corn Salad

*(Ready in about 15 minutes + chilling time | Servings 3)*
**Per serving:** 205 Calories; 9.5g Fat; 27g Carbs; 7.5g Protein; 7.9g Sugars

*Ingredients*
2 ears of corn, husked
3 tablespoons sour cream
1/4 cup plain yogurt
1 garlic clove, minced
1 jalapeño pepper, seeded and minced
1 tablespoon fresh lemon juice
Pink salt and white pepper, to your liking
1 shallot, chopped
2 bell peppers, seeded and thinly sliced
2 tablespoons fresh parsley, chopped
1/4 cup Queso Fresco, crumbled

*Directions*

Start by preheating the Air Fryer to 390 degrees F. Spritz the Air Fryer grill pan with cooking spray.

Place the corn on the grill pan and cook for 10 minutes, turning over halfway through the cooking time. Set aside.

Once the corn has cooled to the touch, use a sharp knife to cut off the kernels into a salad bowl. While the corn is resting, whisk the sour cream, yogurt, garlic, jalapeño pepper, fresh lemon juice, salt, and white pepper.

Add the shallot, pepper, and parsley to the salad bowl and toss to combine well. Toss with the sauce and serve topped with cheese. Enjoy!

## Rainbow Vegetable and Parmesan Croquettes

*(Ready in about 40 minutes | Servings 4)*
**Per serving:** 377 Calories; 19.1g Fat; 40.2g Carbs; 12.1g Protein; 3.9g Sugars

### Ingredients
1 pound potatoes, peeled
4 tablespoons milk
2 tablespoons butter
Salt and black pepper, to taste
1/2 teaspoon cayenne pepper
1/2 cup mushrooms, chopped
1/4 cup broccoli, chopped
1 carrot, grated
1 clove garlic, minced
3 tablespoons scallions, minced
2 tablespoons olive oil
1/2 cup all-purpose flour
2 eggs
1/2 cup panko bread crumbs
1/2 cup parmesan cheese, grated

### Directions
In a large saucepan, boil the potatoes for 17 to 20 minutes. Drain the potatoes and mash with the milk, butter, salt, black pepper, and cayenne pepper.

Add the mushrooms, broccoli, carrots, garlic, scallions, and olive oil; stir to combine well. Shape the mixture into patties.

In a shallow bowl, place the flour; beat the eggs in another bowl; in a third bowl, combine the breadcrumbs with the parmesan cheese.

Dip each patty into the flour, followed by the eggs, and then the breadcrumb mixture; press to adhere.

Cook in the preheated Air Fryer at 375 degrees F for 16 minutes, shaking halfway through the cooking time. Bon appétit!

## Crispy Wax Beans with Almonds and Blue Cheese

*(Ready in about 15 minutes | Servings 3)*
**Per serving:** 242 Calories; 16.9g Fat; 16.3g Carbs; 6.8g Protein; 3.5g Sugars

### Ingredients
1 pound wax beans, cleaned
2 tablespoons peanut oil
4 tablespoons seasoned breadcrumbs
Sea salt and ground black pepper, to taste
1/2 teaspoon red pepper flakes, crushed
2 tablespoons almonds, sliced
1/3 cup blue cheese, crumbled

### Directions
Toss the wax beans with the peanut oil, breadcrumbs, salt, black pepper, and red pepper. Place the wax beans in the lightly greased cooking basket.

Cook in the preheated Air Fryer at 400 degrees F for 5 minutes. Shake the basket once or twice. Add the almonds and cook for 3 minutes more or until lightly toasted. Serve topped with blue cheese and enjoy!

# Indian Malai Kofta

*(Ready in about 40 minutes | Servings 4)*
**Per serving:** 338 Calories; 13.1g Fat; 46.8g Carbs; 10.9g Protein; 9.2g Sugars

### Ingredients

Veggie Balls:

1 pound potatoes, peeled and diced

1/2 pound cauliflower, broken into small florets

2 tablespoons olive oil

2 cloves garlic, minced

1 tablespoon Garam masala

1 cup chickpea flour

Himalayan pink salt and ground black pepper, to taste

Sauce:

1 tablespoon sesame oil

1/2 teaspoon cumin seeds

2 cloves garlic, roughly chopped

1 onion, chopped

1 Kashmiri chili pepper, seeded and minced

1 (1-inch) piece ginger, chopped

1 teaspoon paprika

1 teaspoon turmeric powder

2 ripe tomatoes, pureed

1/2 cup vegetable broth

1/4 full fat coconut milk

### Directions

Start by preheating your Air Fryer to 400 degrees F. Place the potato and cauliflower in a lightly greased cooking basket.

Cook for 15 minutes, shaking the basket halfway through the cooking time. Mash the cauliflower and potatoes in a mixing bowl.

Add the remaining ingredients for the veggie balls and stir to combine well. Shape the vegetable mixture into small balls and arrange them in the cooking basket.

Cook in the preheated Air Fryer at 360 degrees F for 15 minutes or until thoroughly cooked and crispy. Repeat the process until you run out of ingredients.

Heat the sesame oil in a saucepan over medium heat and add the cumin seeds. Once the cumin seeds turn brown, add the garlic, onions, chili pepper, and ginger. Sauté for 2 to 3 minutes.

Add the paprika, turmeric powder, tomatoes, and broth; let it simmer, covered, for 4 to 5 minutes, stirring occasionally.

Add the coconut milk. Heat off; add the veggie balls and gently stir to combine. Bon appétit!

# Carrot and Oat Balls

*(Ready in about 25 minutes | Servings 3)*
**Per serving:** 215 Calories; 4.7g Fat; 37.2g Carbs; 7.5g Protein; 5.6g Sugars

### Ingredients

4 carrots, grated

1 cup rolled oats, ground

1 tablespoon butter, room temperature

1 tablespoon chia seeds

1/2 cup scallions, chopped

2 cloves garlic, minced

2 tablespoons tomato ketchup

1 teaspoon cayenne pepper

1/2 teaspoon sea salt

1/4 teaspoon ground black pepper

1/2 teaspoon ancho chili powder

1/4 cup fresh bread crumbs

### Directions

Start by preheating your Air Fryer to 380 degrees F.

In a bowl, mix all ingredients until everything is well incorporated. Shape the batter into bite-sized balls.

Cook the balls for 15 minutes, shaking the basket halfway through the cooking time. Bon appétit!

# Sweet Potato and Chickpea Tacos

*(Ready in about 15 minutes | Servings 4)*

**Per serving:** 427 Calories; 26.6g Fat; 34.4g Carbs; 15.3g Protein; 4.5g Sugars

### *Ingredients*

2 cups sweet potato puree

2 tablespoons butter, melted

14 ounces canned chickpeas, rinsed

1 cup Colby cheese, shredded

1 teaspoon garlic powder

1 teaspoon onion powder

Salt and freshly cracked black pepper, to taste

8 corn tortillas

1/4 cup Pico de gallo

2 tablespoons fresh coriander, chopped

### *Directions*

Mix the sweet potatoes with the butter, chickpeas, cheese, garlic powder, onion powder, salt, black pepper.

Divide the sweet potato mixture between the tortillas. Bake in the preheated Air Fryer at 390 degrees F for 7 minutes.

Garnish with Pico de gallo and coriander. Bon appétit!

# Kid-Friendly Veggie Tots

*(Ready in about 20 minutes | Servings 4)*

**Per serving:** 222 Calories; 14.2g Fat; 18.3g Carbs; 5.7g Protein; 3.5g Sugars

### *Ingredients*

1 zucchini, grated

1 parsnip, grated

1 carrot, grated

1 onion, chopped

1 garlic clove, minced

2 tablespoons ground flax seeds

2 eggs, whisked

1/2 cup tortilla chips, crushed

1/4 cup pork rinds

Sea salt and ground black pepper, to taste

### *Directions*

Start by preheating your Air Fryer to 400 degrees F.

Then, in a mixing bowl, thoroughly combine all ingredients until everything is well combined. Form the mixture into tot shapes and place in the lightly greased cooking basket.

Bake for 9 to 12 minutes, flipping halfway through, until golden brown around the edges. Bon appétit!

# Quick Shrimp and Vegetable Bake

*(Ready in about 25 minutes | Servings 4)*

**Per serving:** 269 Calories; 8.8g Fat; 21.7g Carbs; 28.2g Protein; 12g Sugars

### *Ingredients*

1 pound shrimp cleaned and deveined

1 cup broccoli, cut into florets

1 cup cauliflower, cut into florets

1 carrot, sliced

2 bell pepper, sliced

1 shallot, sliced

2 tablespoons sesame oil

1 cup tomato paste

### *Directions*

Start by preheating your Air Fryer to 360 degrees F. Spritz the baking pan with cooking spray.

Now, arrange the shrimp and vegetables in the baking pan. Then, drizzle the sesame oil over the vegetables. Pour the tomato paste over the vegetables.

Cook for 10 minutes in the preheated Air Fryer. Stir with a large spoon and cook for a further 12 minutes. Serve warm.

# Roasted Brussels Sprout Salad

*(Ready in about 35 minutes + chilling time | Servings 2)*

**Per serving:** 316 Calories; 16.6g Fat; 33.2g Carbs; 13.8g Protein; 17.7g Sugars

*Ingredients*

1/2 pound Brussels sprouts

1 tablespoon olive oil

Coarse sea salt and ground black pepper, to taste

2 ounces baby arugula

1 shallot, thinly sliced

2 ounces pancetta, chopped

Lemon Vinaigrette:

2 tablespoons extra virgin olive oil

2 tablespoons fresh lemon juice

1 tablespoon honey

1 teaspoon Dijon mustard

*Directions*

Start by preheating your Air Fryer to 380 degrees F.

Add the Brussels sprouts to the cooking basket. Brush with olive oil and cook for 15 minutes. Let it cool to room temperature about 15 minutes.

Toss the Brussels sprouts with the salt, black pepper, baby arugula, and shallot.

Mix all ingredients for the dressing. Then, dress your salad, garnish with pancetta, and serve well chilled. Bon appétit!

# Winter Bliss Bowl

*(Ready in about 45 minutes | Servings 3)*

**Per serving:** 387 Calories; 25.3g Fat; 38.5g Carbs; 6g Protein; 5.8g Sugars

*Ingredients*

1 cup pearled barley

1 (1-pound) head cauliflower, broken into small florets

Coarse sea salt and ground black pepper, to taste

2 tablespoons champagne vinegar

4 tablespoons mayonnaise

1 teaspoon yellow mustard

4 tablespoons olive oil, divided

10 ounces ounce canned sweet corn, drained

2 tablespoons cilantro leaves, chopped

*Directions*

Cook the barley in a saucepan with salted water. Bring to a boil and cook approximately 28 minutes. Drain and reserve.

Start by preheating the Air Fryer to 400 degrees F.

Place the cauliflower florets in the lightly greased Air Fryer basket. Season with salt and black pepper; cook for 12 minutes, tossing halfway through the cooking time.

Toss with the reserved barley. Add the champagne vinegar, mayonnaise, mustard, olive oil, and corn. Garnish with fresh cilantro. Bon appétit!

# Tater Tot Vegetable Casserole

*(Ready in about 40 minutes | Servings 6)*

**Per serving:** 493 Calories; 26.1g Fat; 49.6g Carbs; 17.1g Protein; 5.7g Sugars

*Ingredients*

1 tablespoon olive oil

1 shallot, sliced

2 cloves garlic, minced

1 red bell pepper, seeded and sliced

1 yellow bell pepper, seeded and sliced

1 ½ cups kale

1 (28-ounce) bag frozen tater tots

6 eggs

1 cup milk

Sea salt and ground black pepper, to your liking

1 cup Swiss cheese, shredded

4 tablespoons seasoned breadcrumbs

### Directions

Heat the olive oil in a saucepan over medium-high heat. Sauté the shallot, garlic, and peppers for 2 to 3 minutes. Add the kale and cook until wilted.

Arrange the tater tots evenly over the bottom of a lightly greased casserole dish. Spread the sautéed mixture over the top.

In a mixing bowl, thoroughly combine the eggs, milk, salt, pepper, and shredded cheese. Pour the mixture into the casserole dish.

Lastly, top with the seasoned breadcrumbs. Bake at 330 degrees F for 30 minutes or until top is golden brown. Bon appétit!

## Fried Asparagus with Goat Cheese

*(Ready in about 15 minutes | Servings 3)*

**Per serving:** 132 Calories; 11.2g Fat; 2.2g Carbs; 6.5g Protein; 1g Sugars

### Ingredients

1 bunch of asparagus, trimmed
1 tablespoon olive oil
1/2 teaspoon kosher salt
1/4 teaspoon cracked black pepper, to taste
1/2 teaspoon dried dill weed
1/2 cup goat cheese, crumbled

### Directions

Place the asparagus spears in the lightly greased cooking basket. Toss the asparagus with the olive oil, salt, black pepper, and dill.

Cook in the preheated Air Fryer at 400 degrees F for 9 minutes.

Serve garnished with goat cheese. Bon appétit!

## Cheesy Crusted Baked Eggplant

*(Ready in about 45 minutes | Servings 3)*

**Per serving:** 233 Calories; 7.6g Fat; 29.3g Carbs; 12.9g Protein; 7.4g Sugars

### Ingredients

1 pound eggplant, sliced
1 tablespoon sea salt
1/4 cup Romano cheese, preferably freshly grated
1/3 cup breadcrumbs
Sea salt and cracked black pepper, to taste
1 egg, whisked
4 tablespoons cornmeal
1/4 cup mozzarella cheese, grated
2 tablespoons fresh Italian parsley, roughly chopped

### Directions

Toss the eggplant with 1 tablespoon of salt and let it stand for 30 minutes. Drain and rinse.

Mix the cheese, breadcrumbs, salt, and black pepper in a bowl. Then, add the whisked egg and cornmeal.

Dip the eggplant slices in the batter and press to coat on all sides. Transfer to the lightly greased Air Fryer basket.

Cook at 370 degrees F for 7 to 9 minutes. Turn each slice over and top with the mozzarella. Cook an additional 2 minutes or until the cheese melts. Serve garnished with fresh Italian parsley. Bon appétit!

# Asian Fennel and Noodle Salad

*(Ready in about 20 minutes + chilling time | Servings 3)*

**Per serving:** 248 Calories; 13.2g Fat; 29.9g Carbs; 3.7g Protein; 12.7g Sugars

*Ingredients*

1 fennel bulb, quartered

Salt and white pepper, to taste

1 clove garlic, finely chopped

1 green onion, thinly sliced

2 cups Chinese cabbage, shredded

2 tablespoons rice wine vinegar

1 tablespoon honey

2 tablespoons sesame oil

1 teaspoon ginger, freshly grated

1 tablespoon soy sauce

1 cup chow mein noodles, for serving

*Directions*

Start by preheating your Air Fryer to 370 degrees F.

Now, cook the fennel bulb in the lightly greased cooking basket for 15 minutes, shaking the basket once or twice.

Let it cool completely and toss with the remaining ingredients. Serve well chilled.

# Italian Peperonata Classica

*(Ready in about 25 minutes | Servings 4)*

**Per serving:** 389 Calories; 18.4g Fat; 49.1g Carbs; 9.3g Protein; 19.8g Sugars

*Ingredients*

2 tablespoons olive oil

4 bell peppers, seeded and sliced

1 serrano pepper, seeded and sliced

1/2 cup onion, peeled and sliced

2 garlic cloves, crushed

2 tomatoes, pureed

2 tablespoons tomato ketchup

Sea salt and black pepper

1 teaspoon cayenne pepper

4 fresh basil leaves

10 Sicilian olives green, pitted and sliced

2 Ciabatta rolls

*Directions*

Brush the sides and bottom of the cooking basket with 1 tablespoon of olive oil. Add the peppers, onions, and garlic to the cooking basket. Cook for 5 minutes or until tender.

Add the tomatoes, ketchup, salt, black pepper, and cayenne pepper; add the remaining tablespoon of olive oil and cook in the preheated Air Fryer at 380 degrees F for 15 minutes, stirring occasionally.

Divide between individual bowls and garnish with basil leaves and olives. Serve with the Ciabatta rolls. Bon appétit!

# Cheesy Scalloped Potatoes

*(Ready in about 45 minutes | Servings 4)*

**Per serving:** 470 Calories; 22g Fat; 50.1g Carbs; 18.6g Protein; 8.7g Sugars

*Ingredients*

4 medium potatoes

2 tablespoons butter

2 tablespoons all-purpose flour

1 cup milk

1 cup half-and-half

Sea salt and red pepper flakes, to taste

1/2 teaspoon shallot powder

1/2 teaspoon garlic powder

1 ½ cups Colby cheese, shredded

*Directions*

Bring a large pot of water to a boil. Cook the whole potatoes for about 20 minutes. Drain the potatoes and let sit until cool enough to handle.

Peel your potatoes and slice into 1/8-inch rounds. Melt the butter in a pan over a moderate flame; add the flour and cook for 1 minute. Slowly and gradually, whisk in the milk; cook until the sauce has thickened.

Add the half-and-half, salt, red pepper, shallot powder, and garlic powder.

Place 1/2 of the potatoes overlapping in a single layer in the lightly greased casserole dish. Spoon 1/2 of the cheese sauce on top of the potatoes. Repeat the layers.

Top with the shredded cheese. Bake in the preheated Air Fryer at 325 degrees F for 20 minutes. Serve warm.

# Twice-Baked Potatoes with Pancetta

*(Ready in about 30 minutes | Servings 5)*

**Per serving:** 401 Calories; 7.7g Fat; 69.9g Carbs; 15.2g Protein; 3.8g Sugars

### Ingredients

2 teaspoons canola oil

5 large russet potatoes, peeled

Sea salt and ground black pepper, to taste

5 slices pancetta, chopped

5 tablespoons Swiss cheese, shredded

### Directions

Start by preheating your Air Fryer to 360 degrees F.

Drizzle the canola oil all over the potatoes. Place the potatoes in the Air Fryer basket and cook approximately 20 minutes, shaking the basket periodically.

Lightly crush the potatoes to split and season them with salt and ground black pepper. Add the pancetta and cheese.

Place in the preheated Air Fryer and bake an additional 5 minutes or until cheese has melted. Bon appétit!

# Charred Asparagus and Cherry Tomato Salad

*(Ready in about 10 minutes + chilling time | Servings 4)*

**Per serving:** 289 Calories; 16.7g Fat; 30.1g Carbs; 8.9g Protein; 19.9g Sugars

### Ingredients

1/4 cup olive oil

1 pound asparagus, trimmed

1 pound cherry tomatoes

1/4 cup balsamic vinegar

2 garlic cloves, minced

2 scallion stalks, chopped

1/2 teaspoon oregano

Coarse sea salt and ground black pepper, to your liking

2 hard-boiled eggs, sliced

### Directions

Start by preheating your Air Fryer to 400 degrees F. Brush the cooking basket with 1 tablespoon of olive oil.

Add the asparagus and cherry tomatoes to the cooking basket. Drizzle 1 tablespoon of olive oil all over your veggies.

Cook for 5 minutes, shaking the basket halfway through the cooking time. Let it cool slightly.

Toss with the remaining olive oil, balsamic vinegar, garlic, scallions, oregano, salt, and black pepper.

Afterwards, add the hard-boiled eggs on the top of your salad and serve.

# Skinny Breaded Baby Portabellas

*(Ready in about 15 minutes | Servings 4)*
**Per serving:** 260 Calories; 6.4g Fat; 39.2g Carbs; 12.1g Protein; 5.8g Sugars

*Ingredients*
1 ½ pounds baby portabellas
1/2 cup cornmeal
1/2 cup all-purpose flour
2 eggs
2 tablespoons milk
1 cup breadcrumbs
Sea salt and ground black pepper
1/2 teaspoon shallot powder
1 teaspoon garlic powder
1/2 teaspoon cumin powder
1/2 teaspoon cayenne pepper

*Directions*
Pat the mushrooms dry with a paper towel.
To begin, set up your breading station. Mix the cornmeal and all-purpose flour in a shallow dish.
In a separate dish, whisk the eggs with milk.
Finally, place your breadcrumbs and seasonings in the third dish.
Start by dredging the baby portabellas in the flour mixture; then, dip them into the egg wash. Press the baby portabellas into the breadcrumbs, coating evenly.

Spritz the Air Fryer basket with cooking oil. Add the baby portabellas and cook at 400 degrees F for 6 minutes, flipping them halfway through the cooking time. Bon appétit!

# Crispy Parmesan Asparagus

*(Ready in about 20 minutes | Servings 4)*
**Per serving:** 207 Calories; 12.4g Fat; 11.7g Carbs; 12.2g Protein; 1.6g Sugars

*Ingredients*
2 eggs
1 teaspoon Dijon mustard
1 cup Parmesan cheese, grated
1 cup bread crumbs
Sea salt and ground black pepper, to taste
18 asparagus spears, trimmed
1/2 cup sour cream

*Directions*
Start by preheating your Air Fryer to 400 degrees F.
In a shallow bowl, whisk the eggs and mustard.
In another shallow bowl, combine the Parmesan cheese, breadcrumbs, salt, and black pepper.
Dip the asparagus spears in the egg mixture, then in the parmesan mixture; press to adhere.
Cook for 5 minutes; work in three batches. Serve with sour cream on the side. Enjoy!

## Romano Cheese and Broccoli Balls

*(Ready in about 25 minutes | Servings 4)*
**Per serving:** 192 Calories; 15.2g Fat; 2.9g Carbs; 11.5g Protein; 0.6g Sugars

*Ingredients*
1/2 pound broccoli
1/2 cup Romano cheese, grated
2 garlic cloves, minced
1 shallot, chopped
4 eggs, beaten
2 tablespoons butter, at room temperature
1/2 teaspoon paprika
1/4 teaspoon dried basil
Sea salt and ground black pepper, to taste

*Directions*
Add the broccoli to your food processor and pulse until the consistency resembles rice.
Stir in the remaining ingredients; mix until everything is well combined. Shape the mixture into bite-sized balls and transfer them to the lightly greased cooking basket.
Cook in the preheated Air Fryer at 375 degrees F for 16 minutes, shaking halfway through the cooking time. Serve with cocktail sticks and tomato ketchup on the side.

## Summer Meatball Skewers

*(Ready in about 20 minutes | Servings 6)*
**Per serving:** 218 Calories; 13g Fat; 10.7g Carbs; 14.1g Protein; 8.5g Sugars

*Ingredients*
1/2 pound ground pork
1/2 pound ground beef

1 teaspoon dried onion flakes
1 teaspoon fresh garlic, minced
1 teaspoon dried parsley flakes
Salt and black pepper, to taste
1 red pepper, 1-inch pieces
1 cup pearl onions
1/2 cup barbecue sauce

*Directions*
Mix the ground meat with the onion flakes, garlic, parsley flakes, salt, and black pepper. Shape the mixture into 1-inch balls.
Thread the meatballs, pearl onions, and peppers alternately onto skewers.
Microwave the barbecue sauce for 10 seconds.
Cook in the preheated Air Fryer at 380 degrees for 5 minutes. Turn the skewers over halfway through the cooking time. Brush with the sauce and cook for a further 5 minutes. Work in batches.
Serve with the remaining barbecue sauce and enjoy!

## Italian-Style Tomato-Parmesan Crisps

*(Ready in about 20 minutes | Servings 4)*
**Per serving:** 90 Calories; 8.2g Fat; 2.7g Carbs; 1.8g Protein; 1.1g Sugars

*Ingredients*
4 Roma tomatoes, sliced
2 tablespoons olive oil
Sea salt and white pepper, to taste
1 teaspoon Italian seasoning mix
4 tablespoons Parmesan cheese, grated

*Directions*

Start by preheating your Air Fryer to 350 degrees F. Generously grease the Air Fryer basket with nonstick cooking oil.

Toss the sliced tomatoes with the remaining ingredients. Transfer them to the cooking basket without overlapping.

Cook in the preheated Air Fryer for 5 minutes. Shake the cooking basket and cook an additional 5 minutes. Work in batches.

Serve with Mediterranean aioli for dipping, if desired. Bon appétit!

# Green Bean Crisps

*(Ready in about 20 minutes | Servings 4)*

**Per serving:** 164 Calories; 10.2g Fat; 13.1g Carbs; 6.1g Protein; 1.1g Sugars

*Ingredients*

1 egg, beaten

1/4 cup cornmeal

1/4 cup parmesan, grated

1 teaspoon sea salt

1/2 teaspoon red pepper flakes, crushed

1 pound green beans

2 tablespoons grapeseed oil

*Directions*

In a mixing bowl, combine together the egg, cornmeal, parmesan, salt, and red pepper flakes; mix to combine well.

Dip the green beans into the batter and transfer them to the cooking basket. Brush with the grapeseed oil.

Cook in the preheated Air Fryer at 390 degrees F for 4 minutes. Shake the basket and cook for a further 3 minutes. Work in batches.

Taste, adjust the seasonings and serve. Bon appétit!

# Spinach Chips with Chili Yogurt Dip

*(Ready in about 20 minutes | Servings 3)*

**Per serving:** 128 Calories; 12.3g Fat; 3.1g Carbs; 1.8g Protein; 1.2g Sugars

*Ingredients*

3 cups fresh spinach leaves

1 tablespoon extra-virgin olive oil

1 teaspoon sea salt

1/2 teaspoon cayenne pepper

1 teaspoon garlic powder

Chili Yogurt Dip:

1/4 cup yogurt

2 tablespoons mayonnaise

1/2 teaspoon chili powder

*Directions*

Toss the spinach leaves with the olive oil and seasonings.

Bake in the preheated Air Fryer at 350 degrees F for 10 minutes, shaking the cooking basket occasionally.

Bake until the edges brown, working in batches. In the meantime, make the sauce by whisking all ingredients in a mixing dish. Serve immediately.

# Cheesy Zucchini Sticks

*(Ready in about 20 minutes | Servings 2)*

**Per serving:** 197 Calories; 16.6g Fat; 8.7g Carbs; 4.4g Protein; 0.3g Sugars

*Ingredients*

1 zucchini, slice into strips

2 tablespoons mayonnaise

1/4 cup tortilla chips, crushed

1/4 cup Romano cheese, shredded

Sea salt and black pepper, to your liking

1 tablespoon garlic powder

1/2 teaspoon red pepper flakes

*Directions*

Coat the zucchini with mayonnaise.

Mix the crushed tortilla chips, cheese and spices in a shallow dish.

Then, coat the zucchini sticks with the cheese/chips mixture.

Cook in the preheated Air Fryer at 400 degrees F for 12 minutes, shaking the basket halfway through the cooking time.

Work in batches until the sticks are crispy and golden brown. Bon appétit!

# Party Greek Keftedes

*(Ready in about 20 minutes | Servings 6)*

**Per serving:** 208 Calories; 15.8g Fat; 6.1g Carbs; 10.3g Protein; 3.3g Sugars

*Ingredients*

Greek Keftedes:

1/2 pound mushrooms, chopped

1/2 pound pork sausage, chopped

1 teaspoon shallot powder

1 teaspoon granulated garlic

1 teaspoon dried rosemary

1 teaspoon dried basil

1 teaspoon dried oregano

2 eggs

2 tablespoons cornbread crumbs

Tzatziki Dip:

1 Lebanese cucumbers, grated, juice squeezed out

1 cup full-fat Greek yogurt

1 tablespoon fresh lemon juice

1 garlic clove, minced

1 tablespoon extra-virgin olive oil

1/2 teaspoon salt

*Directions*

In a mixing bowl, thoroughly combine all ingredients for the Greek keftedes.

Shape the meat mixture into bite-sized balls.

Cook in the preheated Air Fryer at 380 degrees for 10 minutes, shaking the cooking basket once or twice to ensure even cooking.

Meanwhile, make the tzatziki dip by mixing all ingredients. Serve the keftedes with cocktail sticks and tzatziki dip on the side. Enjoy!

# Loaded Tater Tot Bites

*(Ready in about 20 minutes | Servings 6)*

**Per serving:** 164 Calories; 9.7g Fat; 9.2g Carbs; 9.3g Protein; 0.8g Sugars

*Ingredients*

24 tater tots, frozen

1 cup Swiss cheese, grated

6 tablespoons Canadian bacon, cooked and chopped

1/4 cup Ranch dressing

*Directions*

Spritz the silicone muffin cups with non-stick cooking spray. Now, press the tater tots down into each cup.

Divide the cheese, bacon, and Ranch dressing between tater tot cups.

Cook in the preheated Air Fryer at 395 degrees for 10 minutes. Serve in paper cake cups. Bon appétit!

# Southern Cheese Straws

*(Ready in about 30 minutes | Servings 6)*

**Per serving:** 269 Calories; 19.3g Fat; 16.6g Carbs; 7.4g Protein; 0.1g Sugars

*Ingredients*

1 cup all-purpose flour

Sea salt and ground black pepper, to taste

1/4 teaspoon smoked paprika

1/2 teaspoon celery seeds

4 ounces mature Cheddar, cold, freshly grated

1 sticks butter

*Directions*

Start by preheating your air Fryer to 330 degrees F. Line the Air Fryer basket with parchment paper.

In a mixing bowl, thoroughly combine the flour, salt, black pepper, paprika, and celery seeds.

Then, combine the cheese and butter in the bowl of a stand mixer. Slowly stir in the flour mixture and mix to combine well.

Then, pack the dough into a cookie press fitted with a star disk. Pipe the long ribbons of dough across the parchment paper. Then cut into six-inch lengths.

Bake in the preheated Air Fryer for 15 minutes. Repeat with the remaining dough. Let the cheese straws cool on a rack. You can store them between sheets of parchment in an airtight container. Bon appétit!

# Sea Scallops and Bacon Skewers

*(Ready in about 50 minutes | Servings 6)*

**Per serving:** 138 Calories; 3.6g Fat; 8.3g Carbs; 17.6g Protein; 5.5g Sugars

*Ingredients*

1/2 pound sea scallops

1/2 cup coconut milk

6 ounces orange juice

1 tablespoon vermouth

Sea salt and ground black pepper, to taste

1/2 pound bacon, diced

1 shallot, diced

1 teaspoon garlic powder

1 teaspoon paprika

*Directions*

In a ceramic bowl, place the sea scallops, coconut milk, orange juice, vermouth, salt, and black pepper; let it marinate for 30 minutes.

Assemble the skewers alternating the scallops, bacon, and shallots. Sprinkle garlic powder and paprika all over the skewers.

Bake in the preheated air Fryer at 400 degrees F for 6 minutes. Serve warm and enjoy!

# Blue Cheesy Potato Wedges

*(Ready in about 20 minutes | Servings 4)*

**Per serving:** 157 Calories; 4.9g Fat; 22.1g Carbs; 6g Protein; 1.2g Sugars

*Ingredients*

2 Yukon Gold potatoes, peeled and cut into wedges

2 tablespoons ranch seasoning

Kosher salt, to taste

1/2 cup blue cheese, crumbled

*Directions*

Sprinkle the potato wedges with the ranch seasoning and salt. Grease generously the Air Fryer basket.

Place the potatoes in the cooking basket.

Roast in the preheated Air Fryer at 400 degrees for 12 minutes. Top with the cheese and roast an additional 3 minutes or until cheese begins to melt. Bon appétit!

# Cocktail Sausage and Veggies on a Stick

*(Ready in about 25 minutes | Servings 4)*

**Per serving:** 190 Calories; 6.8g Fat; 18.5g Carbs; 13.3g Protein; 10.3g Sugars

*Ingredients*

16 cocktail sausages, halved

16 pearl onions

1 red bell pepper, cut into 1 ½-inch pieces

1 green bell pepper, cut into 1 ½-inch pieces

Salt and cracked black pepper, to taste

1/2 cup tomato chili sauce

***Directions***

Thread the cocktail sausages, pearl onions, and peppers alternately onto skewers. Sprinkle with salt and black pepper.

Cook in the preheated Air Fryer at 380 degrees for 15 minutes, turning the skewers over once or twice to ensure even cooking.

Serve with the tomato chili sauce on the side. Enjoy!

## Yakitori (Japanese Chicken Skewers)

*(Ready in about 2 hours 15 minutes | Servings 4)*

**Per serving:** 93 Calories; 2.7g Fat; 2.7g Carbs; 12.1g Protein; 1g Sugars

***Ingredients***

1/2 pound chicken tenders, cut bite-sized pieces

1 clove garlic, minced

1 teaspoon coriander seeds

Sea salt and ground pepper, to taste

2 tablespoons Shoyu sauce

2 tablespoons sake

1 tablespoon fresh lemon juice

1 teaspoon sesame oil

***Directions***

Place the chicken tenders, garlic, coriander, salt, black pepper, Shoyu sauce, sake, and lemon juice in a ceramic dish; cover and let it marinate for 2 hours.

Then, discard the marinade and tread the chicken tenders onto bamboo skewers.

Place the skewered chicken in the lightly greased Air Fryer basket. Drizzle sesame oil all over the skewered chicken.

Cook at 360 degrees for 6 minutes. Turn the skewered chicken over; brush with the reserved marinade and cook for a further 6 minutes. Enjoy!

## Spicy Korean Short Ribs

*(Ready in about 35 minutes | Servings 4)*

**Per serving:** 328 Calories; 19.6g Fat; 12.5g Carbs; 26g Protein; 9.1g Sugars

***Ingredients***

1 pound meaty short ribs

1/2 rice vinegar

1/2 cup soy sauce

1 tablespoon brown sugar

1 tablespoons Sriracha sauce

2 garlic cloves, minced

1 tablespoon daenjang (soybean paste)

1 teaspoon kochukaru (chili pepper flakes)

Sea salt and ground black pepper, to taste

1 tablespoon sesame oil

1/4 cup green onions, roughly chopped

***Directions***

Place the short ribs, vinegar, soy sauce, sugar, Sriracha, garlic, and spices in Ziploc bag; let it marinate overnight.

Rub the sides and bottom of the Air Fryer basket with sesame oil. Discard the marinade and transfer the ribs to the prepared cooking basket.

Cook the marinated ribs in the preheated Air Fryer at 365 degrees for 17 minutes. Turn the ribs over, brush with the reserved marinade, and cook an additional 15 minutes.

Garnish with green onions. Bon appétit!

# Crunchy Roasted Pepitas

*(Ready in about 20 minutes | Servings 4)*

**Per serving:** 199 Calories; 17.8g Fat; 4.3g Carbs; 8.8g Protein; 0.3g Sugars

*Ingredients*

2 cups fresh pumpkin seeds with shells

1 tablespoon olive oil

1 teaspoon sea salt

1 teaspoon ground coriander

1 teaspoon cayenne pepper

*Directions*

Toss the pumpkin seeds with the olive oil.

Spread in an even layer in the Air Fryer basket; roast the seeds at 350 degrees F for 15 minutes, shaking the basket every 5 minutes.

Immediately toss the seeds with the salt, coriander, salt, and cayenne pepper. Enjoy!

# Quick and Easy Popcorn

*(Ready in about 20 minutes | Servings 4)*

**Per serving:** 41 Calories; 1.9g Fat; 4.9g Carbs; 1g Protein; 0.6g Sugars

*Ingredients*

2 tablespoons dried corn kernels

1 teaspoon safflower oil

Kosher salt, to taste

1 teaspoon red pepper flakes, crushed

*Directions*

Add the dried corn kernels to the Air Fryer basket; brush with safflower oil.

Cook at 395 degrees F for 15 minutes, shaking the basket every 5 minutes.

Sprinkle with salt and red pepper flakes. Bon appétit!

# Cheddar Cheese Lumpia Rolls

*(Ready in about 20 minutes | Servings 5)*

**Per serving:** 128 Calories; 6.2g Fat; 14g Carbs; 3.7g Protein; 0g Sugars

*Ingredients*

5 ounces mature cheddar cheese, cut into 15 sticks

15 pieces spring roll lumpia wrappers

2 tablespoons sesame oil

*Directions*

Wrap the cheese sticks in the lumpia wrappers. Transfer to the Air Fryer basket. Brush with sesame oil.

Bake in the preheated Air Fryer at 395 degrees for 10 minutes or until the lumpia wrappers turn golden brown. Work in batches.

Shake the Air Fryer basket occasionally to ensure even cooking. Bon appétit!

# Easy and Delicious Pizza Puffs

*(Ready in about 15 minutes | Servings 6)*

**Per serving:** 186 Calories; 12g Fat; 12.4g Carbs; 6.5g Protein; 3.6g Sugars

*Ingredients*

6 ounces crescent roll dough

1/2 cup mozzarella cheese, shredded

3 ounces pepperoni

3 ounces mushrooms, chopped

1 teaspoon oregano

1 teaspoon garlic powder

1/4 cup Marina sauce, for dipping

*Directions*

Unroll the crescent dough. Roll out the dough using a rolling pin; cut into 6 pieces.

Place the cheese, pepperoni, and mushrooms in the center of each pizza puff. Sprinkle with oregano and garlic powder.

Fold each corner over the filling using wet hands. Press together to cover the filling entirely and seal the edges.

Now, spritz the bottom of the Air Fryer basket with cooking oil. Lay the pizza puffs in a single layer in the cooking basket. Work in batches.

Bake at 370 degrees F for 5 to 6 minutes or until golden brown. Serve with the marinara sauce for dipping.

# Red Beet Chips with Pizza Sauce

*(Ready in about 30 minutes | Servings 4)*

**Per serving:** 66 Calories; 3.7g Fat; 7.7g Carbs; 1.2g Protein; 3.8g Sugars

*Ingredients*

2 red beets, thinly sliced

1 tablespoon grapeseed oil

1 teaspoon seasoned salt

1/2 teaspoon ground black pepper

1/4 teaspoon cumin powder

1/2 cup pizza sauce

*Directions*

Toss the red beets with the oil, salt, black pepper, and cumin powder.

Arrange the beet slices in a single layer in the Air Fryer basket.

Cook in the preheated Air Fryer at 330 degrees F for 13 minutes. Serve with the pizza sauce and enjoy!

# Paprika Zucchini Bombs with Goat Cheese

*(Ready in about 20 minutes | Servings 4)*

**Per serving:** 201 Calories; 9.5g Fat; 16.5g Carbs; 12.7g Protein; 1.2g Sugars

*Ingredients*

1 cup zucchini, grated, juice squeezed out

1 egg

1 garlic clove, minced

1/2 cup all-purpose flour

1/2 cup cornbread crumbs

1/2 cup parmesan cheese, grated

1/2 cup goat cheese, grated

Salt and black pepper, to taste

1 teaspoon paprika

*Directions*

Start by preheating your Air Fryer to 330 degrees F. Spritz the cooking basket with nonstick cooking oil.

Mix all ingredients until everything is well incorporated. Shape the zucchini mixture into golf sized balls and place them in the cooking basket.

Cook in the preheated Air Fryer for 15 to 18 minutes, shaking the basket periodically to ensure even cooking.

Garnish with some extra paprika if desired and serve at room temperature. Bon appétit!

# The Best Party Mix Ever

*(Ready in about 15 minutes | Servings 10)*

**Per serving:** 228 Calories; 12.2g Fat; 24.7g Carbs; 5.9g Protein; 0.6g Sugars

*Ingredients*

2 cups mini pretzels

1 cup mini crackers

1 cup peanuts

1 tablespoon Creole seasoning

2 tablespoons butter, melted

*Directions*

Toss all ingredients in the Air Fryer basket.

Cook in the preheated Air Fryer at 360 degrees F approximately 9 minutes until lightly toasted. Shake the basket periodically. Enjoy!

# Cauliflower Bombs with Sweet & Sour Sauce

*(Ready in about 25 minutes | Servings 4)*
**Per serving:** 156 Calories; 11.9g Fat; 7.2g Carbs; 6.9g Protein; 3.3g Sugars

*Ingredients*
Cauliflower Bombs:
1/2 pound cauliflower
2 ounces Ricotta cheese
1/3 cup Swiss cheese
1 egg
1 tablespoon Italian seasoning mix
Sweet & Sour Sauce:
1 red bell pepper, jarred
1 clove garlic, minced
1 teaspoon sherry vinegar
1 tablespoon tomato puree
2 tablespoons olive oil
Salt and black pepper, to taste

*Directions*
Blanch the cauliflower in salted boiling water about 3 to 4 minutes until al dente. Drain well and pulse in a food processor.
Add the remaining ingredients for the cauliflower bombs; mix to combine well.
Bake in the preheated Air Fryer at 375 degrees F for 16 minutes, shaking halfway through the cooking time.
In the meantime, pulse all ingredients for the sauce in your food processor until combined. Season to taste. Serve the cauliflower bombs with the Sweet & Sour Sauce on the side. Bon appétit!

# Crunchy Roasted Chickpeas

*(Ready in about 25 minutes | Servings 4)*
**Per serving:** 226 Calories; 7.7g Fat; 28.4g Carbs; 11.1g Protein; 5g Sugars

*Ingredients*
1 (15-ounce) can chickpeas, drained and patted dry
1 tablespoon sesame oil
1/8 cup Romano cheese, grated
1/4 teaspoon mustard powder
1/2 teaspoon shallot powder
1/2 teaspoon garlic powder
1 teaspoon coriander, minced
1/2 teaspoon red pepper flakes, crushed
Coarse sea salt and ground black pepper, to taste

*Directions*
Toss all ingredients in a mixing bowl.
Roast in the preheated Air Fryer at 380 degrees F for 10 minutes, shaking the basket halfway through the cooking time.
Work in batches. Bon appétit!

# Homemade Apple Chips

*(Ready in about 20 minutes | Servings 4)*
**Per serving:** 92 Calories; 3.4g Fat; 16.4g Carbs; 1.3g Protein; 12g Sugars

*Ingredients*
2 cooking apples, cored and thinly sliced
1 teaspoon peanut oil
1/4 teaspoon ground cloves
1/4 teaspoon ground cinnamon
1 tablespoon smooth peanut butter

*Directions*
Toss the apple slices with the peanut oil.
Bake at 350 degrees F for 5 minutes; shake the basket to ensure even cooking and continue to cook an additional 5 minutes.
Spread each apple slice with a little peanut butter and sprinkle with ground cloves and cinnamon. Bon appétit!

# Mini Turkey and Corn Burritos

*(Ready in about 25 minutes | Servings 6)*

**Per serving:** 242 Calories; 13.6g Fat; 19.9g Carbs; 13.7g Protein; 2.1g Sugars

*Ingredients*

1 tablespoon olive oil

1/2 pound ground turkey

2 tablespoons shallot, minced

1 garlic clove, smashed

1 red bell pepper, seeded and chopped

1 ancho chili pepper, seeded and minced

1/2 teaspoon ground cumin

Sea salt and freshly ground black pepper, to taste

1/3 cup salsa

6 ounces sweet corn kernels

12 (8-inch) tortilla shells

1 tablespoon butter, melted

1/2 cup sour cream, for serving

*Directions*

Heat the olive oil in a sauté pan over medium-high heat. Cook the ground meat and shallots for 3 to 4 minutes.

Add the garlic and peppers and cook an additional 3 minutes or until fragrant. After that, add the spices, salsa, and corn. Stir until everything is well combined.

Place about 2 tablespoons of the meat mixture in the center of each tortilla. Roll your tortillas to seal the edges and make the burritos.

Brush each burrito with melted butter and place them in the lightly greased cooking basket. Bake at 395 degrees F for 10 minutes, turning them over halfway through the cooking time.

Garnish each burrito with a dollop of sour cream and serve.

# Crunchy Asparagus with Mediterranean Aioli

*(Ready in about 50 minutes | Servings 4)*

**Per serving:** 222 Calories; 13.6g Fat; 18.2g Carbs; 7.1g Protein; 1.3g Sugars

*Ingredients*

Crunchy Asparagus:

2 eggs

3/4 cup breadcrumbs

2 tablespoons Parmesan cheese

Sea salt and ground white pepper, to taste

1/2 pound asparagus, cleaned and trimmed

Cooking spray

Mediterranean Aioli:

4 garlic cloves, minced

4 tablespoons olive oil mayonnaise

1 tablespoons lemon juice, freshly squeezed

*Directions*

Start by preheating your Air Fryer to 400 degrees F.

In a shallow bowl, thoroughly combine the eggs, breadcrumbs, Parmesan cheese, salt, and white pepper.

Dip the asparagus spears in the egg mixture; roll to coat well. Cook in the preheated Air Fryer for 5 to 6 minutes; work in two batches.

Place the garlic on a piece of aluminum foil and spritz with cooking spray. Wrap the garlic in the foil.

Cook in the preheated Air Fryer at 400 degrees for 12 minutes. Check the garlic, open the top of the foil and continue to cook for 10 minutes more. Let it cool for 10 to 15 minutes; remove the cloves by squeezing them out of the skins; mash the garlic and add the mayo and fresh lemon juice; whisk until everything is well combined.

Serve the asparagus with the chilled aioli on the side. Bon appétit!

# Party Chicken Pillows

*(Ready in about 20 minutes | Servings 4)*

**Per serving:** 245 Calories; 16.6g Fat; 10.1g Carbs; 14.8g Protein; 3.5g Sugars

### Ingredients

1 teaspoon olive oil

1 cup ground chicken

1 (8-ounces) can Pillsbury Crescent Roll dough

Sea salt and ground black pepper, to taste

1 teaspoon onion powder

1/2 teaspoon garlic powder

4 tablespoons tomato paste

4 ounces cream cheese, at room temperature

2 tablespoons butter, melted

### Directions

Heat the olive oil in a pan over medium-high heat. Then, cook the ground chicken until browned or about 4 minutes.

Unroll the crescent dough. Roll out the dough using a rolling pin; cut into 8 pieces.

Place the browned chicken, salt, black pepper, onion powder, garlic powder, tomato paste, and cheese in the center of each piece.

Fold each corner over the filling using wet hands. Press together to cover the filling entirely and seal the edges.

Now, spritz the bottom of the Air Fryer basket with cooking oil. Lay the chicken pillows in a single layer in the cooking basket. Drizzle the melted butter all over chicken pillows.

Bake at 370 degrees F for 6 minutes or until golden brown. Work in batches. Bon appétit!

# RICE & GRAINS

## Classic Air Fryer Cornbread

*(Ready in about 30 minutes | Servings 4)*

**Per serving:** 455 Calories; 23.9g Fat; 46.1g Carbs; 13.9g Protein; 4.7g Sugars

*Ingredients*

3/4 cup cornmeal

1 cup flour

2 teaspoons baking powder

1/2 tablespoon brown sugar

1/2 teaspoon salt

5 tablespoons butter, melted

3 eggs, beaten

1 cup full-fat milk

*Directions*

Start by preheating your Air Fryer to 370 degrees F. Then, spritz a baking pan with cooking oil.

In a mixing bowl, combine the flour, cornmeal, baking powder, brown sugar, and salt. In a separate bowl, mix the butter, eggs, and milk.

Pour the egg mixture into the dry cornmeal mixture; mix to combine well.

Pour the batter into the baking pan; cover with aluminum foil and poke tiny little holes all over the foil. Now, bake for 15 minutes.

Remove the foil and bake for 10 minutes more. Transfer to a wire rack to cool slightly before cutting and serving. Bon appétit!

## Delicious Sultana Muffins

*(Ready in about 20 minutes | Servings 4)*

**Per serving:** 288 Calories; 9.5g Fat; 44.3g Carbs; 6.7g Protein; 18.5g Sugars

*Ingredients*

1 cup flour

1 teaspoon baking powder

1tablespoon honey 1 egg

1/2 teaspoon star anise, ground

1 teaspoon vanilla extract

1 egg

1/2 cup milk

2 tablespoons melted butter

1 cup dried Sultanas, soaked in 2 tablespoons of rum

*Directions*

Mix all the ingredients until everything is well incorporated. Spritz a silicone muffin tin with cooking spray.

Pour the batter into the silicone muffin tin.

Bake in the preheated Air Fryer at 330 degrees F for 12 to 15 minutes. Rotate the silicone muffin tin halfway through the cooking time to ensure even cooking.

Bon appétit!

## Easy Mexican Burritos

*(Ready in about 25 minutes | Servings 4)*

**Per serving:** 377 Calories; 20.3g Fat; 25.1g Carbs; 22.7g Protein; 1.8g Sugars

*Ingredients*

1 tablespoon olive oil

1 cup ground beef

1 teaspoon fresh garlic, minced

2 tablespoons scallions, chopped

1 habanero pepper, seeded and chopped

2 (8-ounce) cans refrigerated crescent dinner rolls

1/2 cup canned pinto beans, rinsed and drained

1 tablespoon taco seasoning mix

1 cup Colby cheese, shredded

*Directions*

Heat the olive oil in a skillet over medium heat. Now, cook the ground beef, garlic, scallions, and habanero pepper until the beef is no longer pink and the onion is translucent and fragrant.

Separate the crescent dinner rolls into 8 rectangles.

Divide the beef mixture between rectangles; add the pinto beans and taco seasoning mix; top with the shredded cheese. Roll up and pinch the edge to seal.

Place the seam side down on the parchment-lined Air Fryer basket. Bake in the preheated Air Fryer at 355 degrees F for 20 minutes. Bon appétit!

## Beef Taquito Casserole

*(Ready in about 20 minutes | Servings 4)*
**Per serving:** 364 Calories; 19g Fat; 32.8g Carbs; 16g Protein; 2.8g Sugars

*Ingredients*
1/2 (15-ounce) can black beans, drained and rinsed well
1 tablespoon taco seasoning mix
4 ounces mild enchilada sauce
1 cup Mexican cheese blend, shredded
1/2 (20-ounce) box frozen taquitos (chicken and cheese in tortillas)
2 tablespoons fresh chives, roughly chopped

*Directions*
Start by preheating your Air Fryer to 350 degrees F. Spritz the baking pan with cooking spray.

Mix the beans, taco seasoning mix, enchilada sauce and 1/2 cups of shredded cheese in the baking dish.

Top the mixture with taquitos. Bake for 15 minutes. Top with the remaining 1/2 cup of shredded cheese and bake for a further 15 minutes.

Serve garnished with chopped chives. Enjoy!

## Fried Bread Pudding Squares

*(Ready in about 40 minutes | Servings 4)*
**Per serving:** 313 Calories; 7.2g Fat; 50.2g Carbs; 7.8g Protein; 36.3g Sugars

*Ingredients*
6 slices bread, cubed
1 cup sugar
2 cups milk
2 large eggs, beaten
1/2 teaspoon vanilla extract
1/2 teaspoon ground cinnamon
2 tablespoons dark rum
2 tablespoons icing sugar

*Directions*
Place the bread cubes in a lightly greased baking dish. In a mixing bowl, thoroughly combine the sugar, milk, eggs, vanilla, cinnamon, and rum.

Pour the custard over the bread cubes. Let stand for 30 minutes, occasionally pressing with a wide spatula to submerge.

Cook in the preheated Air Fryer at 370 degrees F degrees for 7 minutes; check to ensure even cooking and cook an additional 5 to 6 minutes.

Place your bread pudding in the refrigerator to cool completely; cut into 1 ½-inch squares. Bake at 330 degrees F for 2 minutes in the lightly buttered Air Fryer basket.

Dust with icing sugar and serve. Bon appétit!

# Golden Cornbread Muffins

*(Ready in about 30 minutes | Servings 4)*

**Per serving:** 383 Calories; 18.3g Fat; 48.8g Carbs; 8.1g Protein; 25.6g Sugars

### Ingredients

1/2 cup sorghum flour

1/2 cup yellow cornmeal

1/4 cup white sugar

2 teaspoons baking powder

A pinch of salt

A pinch of grated nutmeg

2 eggs, beaten

1/2 cup milk

4 tablespoons butter, melted

4 tablespoons honey

### Directions

Start by preheating your Air Fryer to 370 degrees F. Then, line the muffin cups with the paper baking cups.

In a mixing bowl, combine the flour, cornmeal, sugar, baking powder, salt, and nutmeg. In a separate bowl, mix the eggs, milk, and butter.

Pour the egg mixture into the dry cornmeal mixture; mix to combine well.

Pour the batter into the prepared muffin cups. Bake for 15 minutes. Rotate the pan and bake for 10 minutes more.

Transfer to a wire rack to cool slightly before cutting and serving. Serve with honey and enjoy!

# Cheese and Bacon Ciabatta Sandwich

*(Ready in about 10 minutes | Servings 2)*

**Per serving:** 504 Calories; 31.4g Fat; 28.5g Carbs; 26.8g Protein; 3.8g Sugars

### Ingredients

2 ciabatta sandwich buns, split

2 tablespoons butter

2 teaspoons Dijon mustard

4 slices Canadian bacon

4 slices Monterey Jack cheese

### Directions

Place the bottom halves of buns, cut sides up in the parchment lined Air Fryer basket.

Spread the butter and mustard on the buns. Top with the bacon and cheese.

Bake in the preheated Air Fryer at 400 degrees F for 3 minutes. Flip the sandwiches over and cook for 3 minutes longer or until the cheese has melted.

Serve with some extra ketchup or salsa sauce. Bon appétit!

# Caprese Mac and Cheese

*(Ready in about 25 minutes | Servings 3)*

**Per serving:** 587 Calories; 13.2g Fat; 69.7g Carbs; 46.5g Protein; 8.2g Sugars

### Ingredients

1/2 pound cavatappi

1 cup cauliflower florets

1 cup milk

2 cups mozzarella cheese, grated

1/2 teaspoon Italian seasoning

Salt and ground black pepper, to taste

2 tomatoes, sliced

1 cup Parmesan cheese, grated

1 tablespoon fresh basil leaves

### Directions

Bring a pot of salted water to a boil over high heat; turn the heat down to medium and add the cavatappi and cauliflower.

Let it simmer about 8 minutes. Drain the cavatappi and cauliflower; place them in a lightly greased baking pan.

Add the milk and mozzarella cheese to the baking pan; gently stir to combine. Add the Italian seasoning, salt, and black pepper.

Top with the tomatoes and parmesan cheese.

Bake in the preheated Air Fryer at 360 degrees F for 15 minutes. Serve garnished with fresh basil leaves. Bon appétit!

# Buckwheat and Potato Flat Bread

*(Ready in about 20 minutes | Servings 4)*

**Per serving:** 334 Calories; 1.2g Fat; 77.3g Carbs; 8.4g Protein; 19.5g Sugars

*Ingredients*

4 potatoes, medium-sized

1 cup buckwheat flour

1/2 teaspoon salt

1/2 teaspoon red chili powder

1/4 cup honey

*Directions*

Put the potatoes into a large saucepan; add water to cover by about 1 inch. Bring to a boil. Then, lower the heat, and let your potatoes simmer about 8 minutes until they are fork tender.

Mash the potatoes and add the flour, salt, and chili powder. Create 4 balls and flatten them with a rolling pin

Bake in the preheated Air Fryer at 390 degrees F for 6 minutes. Serve warm with honey.

# Couscous and Black Bean Bowl

*(Ready in about 35 minutes | Servings 4)*

**Per serving:** 352 Calories; 12g Fat; 49.9g Carbs; 12.6g Protein; 1.7g Sugars

*Ingredients*

1 cup couscous

1 cup canned black beans, drained and rinsed

1 tablespoon fresh cilantro, chopped

1 bell pepper, sliced

2 tomatoes, sliced

2 cups baby spinach

1 red onion, sliced

Sea salt and ground black pepper, to taste

1 teaspoon lemon juice

1 teaspoon lemon zest

1 tablespoon olive oil

4 tablespoons tahini

*Directions*

Put the couscous in a bowl; pour the boiling water to cover by about 1 inch. Cover and set aside for 5 to 8 minutes; fluff with a fork.

Place the couscous in a lightly greased cake pan. Transfer the pan to the Air Fryer basket and cook at 360 digress F about 20 minutes. Make sure to stir every 5 minutes to ensure even cooking.

Transfer the prepared couscous to a mixing bowl. Add the remaining ingredients; gently stir to combine. Bon appétit!

# Delicious Coconut Granola

*(Ready in about 40 minutes | Servings 12)*

**Per serving:** 192 Calories; 7.1g Fat; 36.2g Carbs; 4.3g Protein; 24.8g Sugars

*Ingredients*

2 cups rolled oats

2 tablespoons butter

1 cup honey

1/2 teaspoon coconut extract

1/2 teaspoon vanilla extract

1/4 cup sesame seeds

1/4 cup pumpkin seeds

1/2 cup coconut flakes

*Directions*

Thoroughly combine all ingredients, except the coconut flakes; mix well.

Spread the mixture onto the Air Fryer trays. Spritz with nonstick cooking spray.

Bake at 230 degrees F for 25 minutes; rotate the trays, add the coconut flakes, and bake for a further 10 to 15 minutes.

This granola can be stored in an airtight container for up to 3 weeks. Enjoy!

## Savory Cheesy Cornmeal Biscuits

*(Ready in about 35 minutes | Servings 6)*
**Per serving:** 444 Calories; 26.7g Fat; 37.6g Carbs; 13.4g Protein; 1.6g Sugars

### Ingredients

2 cups all-purpose flour

1 teaspoon baking soda

1 teaspoon baking powder

1 teaspoon granulated sugar

1/4 teaspoon ground chipotle

Sea salt, to taste

A pinch of grated nutmeg

1 stick butter, cold

6 ounces canned whole corn kernels

1 cup Colby cheese, shredded

2 tablespoons sour cream

2 eggs, beaten

### Directions

In a mixing bowl, combine the flour, baking soda, baking powder, sugar, ground chipotle, salt, and a pinch of nutmeg.

Cut in the butter until the mixture resembles coarse crumbs. Stir in the corn, Colby cheese, sour cream, and eggs; stir until everything is well incorporated.

Turn the dough out onto a floured surface. Knead the dough with your hands and roll it out to 1-inch thickness. Using 3-inch round cutter, cut out the biscuits.

Transfer the cornmeal biscuits to the lightly greased Air Fryer basket. Brush the biscuits with cooking oil.

Bake in the preheated Air Fryer at 400 degrees F for 17 minutes. Continue cooking until all the batter is used. Bon appétit!

## Asian-Style Shrimp Pilaf

*(Ready in about 45 minutes | Servings 3)*
**Per serving:** 368 Calories; 5.3g Fat; 68.4g Carbs; 9.9g Protein; 13.9g Sugars

### Ingredients

1 cup koshihikari rice, rinsed

1 yellow onion, chopped

2 garlic cloves, minced

1/2 teaspoon fresh ginger, grated

1 tablespoon Shoyu sauce

2 tablespoons rice wine

1 tablespoon sushi seasoning

1 tablespoon caster sugar

1/2 teaspoon sea salt

5 ounces frozen shrimp, thawed

2 tablespoons katsuobushi flakes, for serving

### Directions

Place the koshihikari rice and 2 cups of water in a large saucepan and bring to a boil. Cover, turn the heat down to low, and continue cooking for 15 minutes more. Set aside for 10 minutes.

Mix the rice, onion, garlic, ginger, Shoyu sauce, wine, sushi seasoning, sugar, and salt in a lightly greased baking dish.

Cook in the preheated Air Fryer at 370 degrees for 13 to 16 minutes.

Add the shrimp to the baking dish and gently stir until everything is well combined. Cook for 6 minutes more.

Serve at room temperature, garnished with katsuobushi flakes. Enjoy!

# Classic Pancakes with Blueberries

*(Ready in about 30 minutes | Servings 4)*

**Per serving:** 331 Calories; 12g Fat; 46.9g Carbs; 8.9g Protein; 21.2g Sugars

*Ingredients*

1 cup flour

1 teaspoon baking powder

1 teaspoon baking soda

1/2 teaspoon salt

1 teaspoon granulated sugar

2 eggs, beaten

1/2 cup milk

2 tablespoons butter melted

4 tablespoons maple syrup

1/2 cup fresh blueberries

*Directions*

Mix the flour, baking powder, baking soda, salt, sugar, and eggs in a large bowl. Gradually add the milk and the melted butter, whisking continuously, until well combined.

Let it stand for 20 minutes.

Spritz the Air Fryer baking pan with cooking spray. Pour the batter into the pan using a measuring cup.

Cook at 230 degrees F for 4 to 5 minutes or until golden brown. Repeat with the remaining batter. Serve with maple syrup and fresh blueberries. Bon appétit!

# Mediterranean Pita Pockets

*(Ready in about 25 minutes | Servings 4)*

**Per serving:** 350 Calories; 10.5g Fat; 42.1g Carbs; 24.9g Protein; 4.2g Sugars

*Ingredients*

1 teaspoon olive oil

1 onion

2 garlic cloves, minced

3/4 pound ground turkey

Salt and ground black pepper, to taste

1/2 teaspoon mustard seeds

4 small pitas

Tzatziki

1/2 cup Greek-style yogurt

1/2 cucumber, peeled

1 clove garlic, minced

2 tablespoons fresh lemon juice

Sea salt, to taste

1/4 teaspoon dried oregano

*Directions*

Mix the olive oil, onion, garlic, turkey, salt, black pepper, and mustard seeds; shape the mixture into four patties.

Cook in the preheated Air Fryer at 370 degrees F for 10 minutes, turning them over once or twice.

Meanwhile, mix all ingredients for the tzatziki and place in the refrigerator until ready to use.

Warm the pita pockets in the preheated Air Fryer at 360 degrees F for 4 to 5 minutes or until thoroughly heated.

Spread the tzatziki in pita pockets and add the turkey patties. Enjoy!

# Grilled Garlic and Avocado Toast

*(Ready in about 15 minutes | Servings 2)*

**Per serving:** 389 Calories; 29.5g Fat; 28.8g Carbs; 5.6g Protein; 2.9g Sugars

*Ingredients*

4 slices artisan bread

1 garlic clove, halved

2 tablespoons olive oil

1 avocado, seeded, peeled and mashed

1/2 teaspoon sea salt

1/4 teaspoon ground black pepper

*Directions*

Rub 1 side of each bread slice with garlic. Brush with olive oil.

Place the bread slices on the Air Fryer grill pan. Bake in the preheated Air Fryer at 400 degrees F for 3 to 4 minutes.

Slather the mashed avocado on top of the toast and season with salt and pepper. Enjoy!

## Stuffed French Toast

*(Ready in about 15 minutes | Servings 3)*

**Per serving:** 430 Calories; 24.1g Fat; 44.1g Carbs; 10.3g Protein; 24g Sugars

*Ingredients*

6 slices of challah bread, without crusts

1/4 cup Mascarpone cheese

3 tablespoons fig jam

1 egg

4 tablespoons milk

1/2 teaspoon grated nutmeg

1 teaspoon ground cinnamon

1/2 teaspoon vanilla paste

1/4 cup butter, melted

1/2 cup brown sugar

*Directions*

Spread the three slices of bread with the mascarpone cheese, leaving 1/2-inch border at the edges.

Spread the three slices of bread with 1/2 tablespoon of fig jam; then, invert them onto the slices with the cheese in order to make sandwiches.

Mix the egg, milk, nutmeg, cinnamon, and vanilla in a shallow dish. Dip your sandwiches in the egg mixture.

Cook in the preheated Air Fryer at 340 degrees F for 4 minutes. Dip in the melted butter, then, roll in the brown sugar. Serve warm.

## Almost Famous Four-Cheese Pizza

*(Ready in about 15 minutes | Servings 4)*

**Per serving:** 551 Calories; 34.3g Fat; 32.7g Carbs; 26.6g Protein; 6.2g Sugars

*Ingredients*

1 (11-ounce) can refrigerated thin pizza crust

1/2 cup tomato pasta sauce

2 tablespoons scallions, chopped

1/4 cup Parmesan cheese, grated

1 cup provolone cheese, shredded

1 cup mozzarella cheese. sliced

4 slices cheddar cheese

1 tablespoon olive oil

*Directions*

Stretch the dough on a work surface lightly dusted with flour. Spread with a layer of tomato pasta sauce.

Top with the scallions and cheese. Place on the baking tray that is previously greased with olive oil.

Bake in the preheated Air Fryer at 395 degrees F for 5 minutes. Rotate the baking tray and bake for a further 5 minutes. Serve immediately.

## Crispy Pork Wontons

*(Ready in about 20 minutes | Servings 3)*

**Per serving:** 296 Calories; 14.5g Fat; 21.8g Carbs; 18.3g Protein; 1.7g Sugars

*Ingredients*

1 tablespoon olive oil

3/4 pound ground pork

1 red bell pepper, seeded and chopped

1 green bell pepper, seeded and chopped

1 habanero pepper, minced

3 tablespoons onion, finely chopped

Salt and ground black pepper, to taste

1/2 teaspoon dried parsley flakes

1 teaspoon dried thyme

6 wonton wrappers

### Directions

Heat the olive oil in a heavy skillet over medium heat. Cook the ground pork, peppers, and onion until tender and fragrant or about 4 minutes.

Add the seasonings and stir to combine.

Lay a piece of the wonton wrapper on your palm; add the filling in the middle of the wrapper. Then, fold it up to form a triangle; pinch the edges to seal tight.

Place the folded wontons in the lightly greased cooking basket. Cook at 360 degrees F for 10 minutes. Work in batches and serve warm. Bon appétit!

## Japanese Yaki Onigiri

*(Ready in about 50 minutes | Servings 2)*

**Per serving:** 603 Calories; 13.3g Fat; 95.8g Carbs; 23.3g Protein; 4.4g Sugars

### Ingredients

1/2 cup sushi rice, cooked

1 cup canned green peas, drained

1/4 cup cream cheese

1/4 cup Colby cheese, shredded

2 tablespoons dashi

Salt and cracked black pepper, to taste

2 tablespoons scallions, chopped

1 cup all-purpose flour

1 egg, whisked

2 tablespoons soy sauce (unagi)

### Directions

In a bowl, combine the rice, green peas, cheese, dashi, salt, black pepper, and scallions. Add the flour and egg and mix to combine well.

Refrigerate for 20 to 40 minutes.

Then, put some salt in your hands and rub to spread all around. Form the rice mixture into triangles.

Cook in the preheated Air Fryer at 370 degrees F for 7 to 10 minutes. Brush with the unagi sauce and serve immediately. Enjoy!

## Mexican Taco Bake

*(Ready in about 40 minutes | Servings 4)*

**Per serving:** 540 Calories; 29.5g Fat; 33.3g Carbs; 34.8g Protein; 7.2g Sugars

### Ingredients

1 tablespoon olive oil

1/4 pound ground beef

1/2 pound ground pork

1 shallot, minced

1 garlic, minced

1/2 cup beef broth

1 bell pepper, seeded and chopped

1 Mexican chili pepper, seeded and minced

1 ½ cups tomato sauce

4 flour tortillas for fajitas

1 cup Mexican cheese blend, shredded

### Directions

Heat the olive oil in a heavy skillet over a moderate flame. Cook the ground meat with the shallots and garlic until no longer pink.

Then, add the beef broth, peppers, and tomato sauce to the skillet. Continue to cook on low heat for 3 minutes, stirring continuously.

Spritz a baking dish with nonstick cooking spray. Cut the tortillas in half; place 2 tortilla halves in the bottom of the baking dish.

Top with half of the meat mixture. Sprinkle with 1/2 cup of the cheese and the remaining tortilla halves. Top with the remaining meat mixture and cheese.

Cover with a piece of aluminum foil and bake in the preheated Air Fryer at 330 degrees F for 20 minutes. Remove the foil and bake for a further 12 minutes or until thoroughly heated. Enjoy!

# Broccoli Bruschetta with Romano Cheese

*(Ready in about 20 minutes | Servings 3)*
**Per serving:** 264 Calories; 14.2g Fat; 24.3g Carbs; 10.4g Protein; 4.9g Sugars

### Ingredients

6 slices of panini bread

1 teaspoon garlic puree

3 tablespoons extra-virgin olive oil

6 tablespoons passata di pomodoro (tomato passata)

1 cup small broccoli florets

1/2 cup Romano cheese, grated

### Directions

Place the slices of panini bread on a flat surface.

In a small mixing bowl, combine together the garlic puree and extra-virgin olive oil. Brush one side of each bread slice with the garlic/oil mixture. Place in the Air Fryer grill pan. Add the tomato passata, broccoli, and cheese.

Cook in the preheated Air Fryer at 370 degrees F for 10 minutes. Bon appétit!

# Polenta Bites with Wild Mushroom Ragout

*(Ready in about 50 minutes | Servings 3)*
**Per serving:** 220 Calories; 16.6g Fat; 12.4g Carbs; 6.8g Protein; 2.2g Sugars

### Ingredients

2 cups water

1 teaspoon salt

1/2 cup polenta

2 tablespoons butter, melted

1 tablespoon olive oil

6 ounces wild mushrooms, sliced

1/2 red onion, chopped

1/2 teaspoon fresh garlic, minced

Sea salt and freshly ground black pepper, to taste

1 teaspoon cayenne pepper

1/2 cup dry white wine

### Directions

Bring 2 cups of water and 1 teaspoon salt to a boil in a saucepan over medium-high heat. Slowly and gradually, stir in the polenta, whisking constantly.

Reduce the heat to medium-low and continue to cook for 5 to 6 minutes more. Stir in the butter and mix to combine. Pour the prepared polenta into a parchment-lined baking pan, cover and let stand for 15 to 20 minutes or until set.

In the meantime, preheat your Air Fryer to 360 degrees F. Heat the olive oil until sizzling. Then, add the mushrooms, onion, and garlic to the baking pan.

Cook for 5 minutes, stirring occasionally. Season with salt, black pepper, cayenne pepper, and wine; cook an additional 5 minutes and reserve.

Cut the polenta into 18 squares. Transfer to the lightly greased cooking basket. Cook in the preheated Air Fryer at 395 degrees F for about 8 minutes.

Top with the wild mushroom ragout and bake an additional 3 minutes. Serve warm.

# Cornmeal Crusted Okra

*(Ready in about 30 minutes | Servings 2)*

**Per serving:** 314 Calories; 10.1g Fat; 49.3g Carbs; 10.3g Protein; 3.2g Sugars

*Ingredients*

3/4 cup cornmeal

1/4 cup parmesan cheese, grated

Sea salt and ground black pepper, to taste

1 teaspoon cayenne pepper

1 teaspoon garlic powder

1/2 teaspoon cumin seeds

1/2 pound of okra, cut into small chunks

2 teaspoons sesame oil

*Directions*

In a mixing bowl, thoroughly combine the cornmeal, parmesan, salt, black pepper, cayenne pepper, garlic powder, and cumin seeds. Stir well to combine.

Roll the okra pods over the cornmeal mixture, pressing to adhere. Drizzle with sesame oil.

Cook in the preheated Air Fryer at 370 digress F for 20 minutes, shaking the basket periodically to ensure even cooking. Bon appétit!

# Tex Mex Pasta Bake

*(Ready in about 40 minutes | Servings 4)*

**Per serving:** 666 Calories; 27.7g Fat; 72.2g Carbs; 42.3g Protein; 4.3g Sugars

*Ingredients*

3/4 pound pasta noodles

1 tablespoon olive oil

3/4 pound ground beef

1 medium-sized onion, chopped

1 teaspoon fresh garlic, minced

1 bell pepper, seeded and sliced

1 jalapeno, seeded and minced

Sea salt and cracked black pepper, to taste

1 ½ cups enchilada sauce

1 cup Mexican cheese blend, shredded

1/3 cup tomato paste

1/2 teaspoon Mexican oregano

1/2 cup nacho chips

2 tablespoons fresh coriander, chopped

*Directions*

Boil the pasta noodles for 3 minutes less than mentioned on the package; drain, rinse and place in the lightly greased casserole dish.

In a saucepan, heat the olive oil until sizzling. Add the ground beef and cook for 2 to 3 minutes or until slightly brown.

Now, add the onion, garlic, and peppers and continue to cook until tender and fragrant or about 2 minutes. Season with salt and black pepper.

Add the enchilada sauce to the casserole dish. Add the beef mixture and 1/2 cup of the Mexican cheese blend. Gently stir to combine.

Add the tomato paste, Mexican oregano, nacho chips, and the remaining 1/2 cup of cheese blend. Cover with foil.

Bake in the preheated Air Fryer at 350 degrees F for 20 minutes; remove the foil and bake for a further 10 to 12 minutes. Serve garnished with fresh coriander and enjoy!

# Tyrolean Kaiserschmarrn (Austrian Pancakes)

*(Ready in about 30 minutes | Servings 4)*
**Per serving:** 370 Calories; 5.8g Fat; 72.3g Carbs; 10.2g Protein; 48.2g Sugars

### Ingredients
1/2 cup flour
A pinch of salt
A pinch of sugar
1/2 cup whole milk
3 eggs
1 shot of rum
4 tablespoons raisins
1/2 cup icing sugar
1/2 cup stewed plums

### Directions
Mix the flour, salt, sugar, and milk in a bowl until the batter becomes semi-solid.

Fold in the eggs; add the rum and whisk to combine well. Let it stand for 20 minutes.

Spritz the Air Fryer baking pan with cooking spray. Pour the batter into the pan using a measuring cup. Scatter the raisins over the top.

Cook at 230 degrees F for 4 to 5 minutes or until golden brown. Repeat with the remaining batter. Cut the pancake into pieces, sprinkle over the icing sugar, and serve with the stewed plums. Bon appétit!

# VEGAN

## Corn on the Cob with Spicy Avocado Spread

*(Ready in about 15 minutes | Servings 4)*
**Per serving:** 234 Calories; 9.2g Fat; 37.9g Carbs; 7.2g Protein; 1.9g Sugars

*Ingredients*
4 corn cobs
1 avocado, pitted, peeled and mashed
1 clove garlic, pressed
1 tablespoon fresh lime juice
1 tablespoon soy sauce
4 teaspoons nutritional yeast
1/2 teaspoon cayenne pepper
1/2 teaspoon dried dill
Sea salt and ground black pepper, to taste
1 teaspoon hot sauce
2 heaping tablespoons fresh cilantro leaves, roughly chopped

*Directions*
Spritz the corn with cooking spray. Cook at 390 degrees F for 6 minutes, turning them over halfway through the cooking time.
In the meantime, mix the avocado, lime juice, soy sauce, nutritional yeast, cayenne pepper, dill, salt, black pepper, and hot sauce.
Spread the avocado mixture all over the corn on the cob. Garnish with fresh cilantro leaves. Bon appétit!

## Delicious Asparagus and Mushroom Fritters

*(Ready in about 15 minutes | Servings 4)*
**Per serving:** 231 Calories; 12.7g Fat; 24g Carbs; 10.2g Protein; 6.3g Sugars

*Ingredients*
1 pound asparagus spears
1 tablespoon canola oil
1 teaspoon paprika
Sea salt and freshly ground black pepper, to taste
1 teaspoon garlic powder
3 tablespoons scallions, chopped
1 cup button mushrooms, chopped
1/2 cup fresh breadcrumbs
1 tablespoon flax seeds, soaked in 2 tablespoons of water (vegan "egg")
4 tablespoons sun-dried tomato hummus

*Directions*
Place the asparagus spears in the lightly greased cooking basket. Toss the asparagus with the canola oil, paprika, salt, and black pepper.
Cook in the preheated Air Fryer at 400 degrees F for 5 minutes. Chop the asparagus spears and add the garlic powder, scallions, mushrooms, breadcrumbs, and vegan "egg".
Mix until everything is well incorporated and form the asparagus mixture into patties.
Cook in the preheated Air Fryer at 400 degrees F for 5 minutes, flipping halfway through the cooking time. Serve with sun-dried tomato hummus. Bon appétit!

## Greek-Style Roasted Vegetables

*(Ready in about 25 minutes | Servings 3)*
**Per serving:** 299 Calories; 12.9g Fat; 30.4g Carbs; 5.8g Protein; 12.5g Sugars

*Ingredients*
1/2 pound butternut squash, peeled and cut into 1-inch chunks
1/2 pound cauliflower, cut into 1-inch florets

1/2 pound zucchini, cut into 1-inch chunks

1 red onion, sliced

2 bell peppers, cut into 1-inch chunks

2 tablespoons extra-virgin olive oil

1 cup dry white wine

1 teaspoon dried rosemary

Sea salt and freshly cracked black pepper, to taste

1/2 teaspoon dried basil

1 (28-ounce) canned diced tomatoes with juice

1/2 cup Kalamata olives, pitted

***Directions***

Toss the vegetables with the olive oil, wine, rosemary, salt, black pepper, and basil until well coated.

Pour 1/2 of the canned diced tomatoes into a lightly greased baking dish; spread to cover the bottom of the baking dish.

Add the vegetables and top with the remaining diced tomatoes. Scatter the Kalamata olives over the top.

Bake in the preheated Air Fryer at 390 degrees F for 20 minutes, rotating the dish halfway through the cooking time. Serve warm and enjoy!

# Warm Farro Salad with Roasted Tomatoes

*(Ready in about 40 minutes | Servings 2)*

**Per serving:** 452 Calories; 14.5g Fat; 72.9g Carbs; 7.7g Protein; 9.5g Sugars

***Ingredients***

3/4 cup farro

3 cups water

1 tablespoon sea salt

1 pound cherry tomatoes

2 spring onions, chopped

2 carrots, grated

2 heaping tablespoons fresh parsley leaves

2 tablespoons champagne vinegar

2 tablespoons white wine

2 tablespoons extra-virgin olive oil

1 teaspoon red pepper flakes

***Directions***

Place the farro, water, and salt in a saucepan and bring it to a rapid boil. Turn the heat down to medium-low, and simmer, covered, for 30 minutes or until the farro has softened.

Drain well and transfer to an air fryer-safe pan. Meanwhile, place the cherry tomatoes in the lightly greased Air Fryer basket. Roast at 400 degrees F for 4 minutes.

Add the roasted tomatoes to the pan with the cooked farro, Toss the salad ingredients with the spring onions, carrots, parsley, vinegar, white wine, and olive oil.

Bake at 360 degrees F an additional 5 minutes. Serve garnished with red pepper flakes and enjoy!

# Winter Squash and Tomato Bake

*(Ready in about 30 minutes | Servings 4)*

**Per serving:** 330 Calories; 25.3g Fat; 23.2g Carbs; 8.5g Protein; 3.2g Sugars

***Ingredients***

Cashew Cream:

1/2 cup sunflower seeds, soaked overnight, rinsed and drained

1/4 cup lime juice

Sea salt, to taste

2 teaspoons nutritional yeast

1 tablespoon tahini

1/2 cup water

Squash:

1 pound winter squash, peeled and sliced

2 tablespoons olive oil

Sea salt and ground black pepper, to taste

Sauce:

2 tablespoons olive oil

2 ripe tomatoes, crushed

6 ounces spinach, torn into small pieces

2 garlic cloves, minced

1 cup vegetable broth

1/2 teaspoon dried rosemary

1/2 teaspoon dried basil

*Directions*

Mix the ingredients for the cashew cream in your food processor until creamy and uniform. Reserve.

Place the squash slices in the lightly greased casserole dish. Add the olive oil, salt, and black pepper.

Mix all the ingredients for the sauce. Pour the sauce over the vegetables. Bake in the preheated Air Fryer at 390 degrees F for 15 minutes.

Top with the cashew cream and bake an additional 5 minutes or until everything is thoroughly heated.

Transfer to a wire rack to cool slightly before sling and serving.

# Mashed Potatoes with Roasted Peppers

*(Ready in about 1 hour | Servings 4)*

**Per serving:** 490 Calories; 17g Fat; 79.1g Carbs; 10.5g Protein; 9.8g Sugars

*Ingredients*

4 potatoes

1 tablespoon vegan margarine

1 teaspoon garlic powder

1 pound bell peppers, seeded and quartered lengthwise

2 Fresno peppers, seeded and halved lengthwise

4 tablespoons olive oil

2 tablespoons cider vinegar

4 garlic cloves, pressed

Kosher salt, to taste

1/2 teaspoon freshly ground black pepper

1/2 teaspoon dried dill

*Directions*

Place the potatoes in the Air Fryer basket and cook at 400 degrees F for 40 minutes. Discard the skin and mash the potatoes with the vegan margarine and garlic powder.

Then, roast the peppers at 400 degrees F for 5 minutes. Give the peppers a half turn; place them back in the cooking basket and roast for another 5 minutes.

Turn them one more time and roast until the skin is charred and soft or 5 more minutes. Peel the peppers and let them cool to room temperature.

Toss your peppers with the remaining ingredients and serve with the mashed potatoes. Bon appétit!

# Hungarian Mushroom Pilaf

*(Ready in about 50 minutes | Servings 4)*

**Per serving:** 566 Calories; 19.1g Fat; 72.8g Carbs; 24.6g Protein; 7.2g Sugars

*Ingredients*

1 ½ cups white rice

3 cups vegetable broth

2 tablespoons olive oil

1 pound fresh porcini mushrooms, sliced

2 tablespoons olive oil

2 garlic cloves

1 onion, chopped

1/4 cup dry vermouth

1 teaspoon dried thyme

1/2 teaspoon dried tarragon

1 teaspoon sweet Hungarian paprika

*Directions*

Place the rice and broth in a large saucepan, add water; and bring to a boil. Cover, turn the heat down to low, and continue cooking for 16 to 18 minutes more. Set aside for 5 to 10 minutes.

Now, stir the hot cooked rice with the remaining ingredients in a lightly greased baking dish.

Cook in the preheated Air Fryer at 370 degrees for 20 minutes, checking periodically to ensure even cooking.

Serve in individual bowls. Bon appétit!

## Rosemary Au Gratin Potatoes

*(Ready in about 45 minutes | Servings 4)*

**Per serving:** 386 Calories; 15.7g Fat; 50.5g Carbs; 14.3g Protein; 6.1g Sugars

*Ingredients*

2 pounds potatoes

1/4 cup sunflower kernels, soaked overnight

1/2 cup almonds, soaked overnight

1 cup unsweetened almond milk

2 tablespoons nutritional yeast

1 teaspoon shallot powder

2 fresh garlic cloves, minced

1/2 cup water

Kosher salt and ground black pepper, to taste

1 teaspoon cayenne pepper

1 tablespoon fresh rosemary

*Directions*

Bring a large pan of water to a boil. Cook the whole potatoes for about 20 minutes. Drain the potatoes and let sit until cool enough to handle.

Peel your potatoes and slice into 1/8-inch rounds. Add the sunflower kernels, almonds, almond milk, nutritional yeast, shallot powder, and garlic to your food processor; blend until uniform, smooth, and creamy. Add the water and blend for 30 seconds more.

Place 1/2 of the potatoes overlapping in a single layer in the lightly greased casserole dish. Spoon 1/2 of the sauce on top of the potatoes. Repeat the layers, ending with the sauce.

Top with salt, black pepper, cayenne pepper, and fresh rosemary. Bake in the preheated Air Fryer at 325 degrees F for 20 minutes. Serve warm.

## Kid-Friendly Vegetable Fritters

*(Ready in about 20 minutes | Servings 4)*

**Per serving:** 299 Calories; 11.3g Fat; 44.1g Carbs; 7.9g Protein; 4.6g Sugars

*Ingredients*

1 pound broccoli florets

1 tablespoon ground flaxseeds

1 yellow onion, finely chopped

1 sweet pepper, seeded and chopped

1 carrot, grated

2 garlic cloves, pressed

1 teaspoon turmeric powder

1/2 teaspoon ground cumin

1/2 cup all-purpose flour

1/2 cup cornmeal

Salt and ground black pepper, to taste

2 tablespoons olive oil

*Directions*

Blanch the broccoli in salted boiling water until al dente, about 3 to 4 minutes. Drain well and transfer to a mixing bowl; mash the broccoli florets with the remaining ingredients.

Form the mixture into patties and place them in the lightly greased Air Fryer basket.

Cook at 400 degrees F for 6 minutes, turning them over halfway through the cooking time; work in batches.

Serve warm with your favorite Vegenaise. Enjoy!

# Marinated Tofu Bowl with Pearl Onions

*(Ready in about 1 hour 20 minutes | Servings 4)*
**Per serving:** 296 Calories; 16.7g Fat; 23.2g Carbs; 18.1g Protein; 14.1g Sugars

*Ingredients*
16 ounces firm tofu, pressed and cut into 1-inch pieces
2 tablespoons vegan Worcestershire sauce
1 tablespoon apple cider vinegar
1 tablespoon maple syrup
1/2 teaspoon shallot powder
1/2 teaspoon porcini powder
1/2 teaspoon garlic powder
2 tablespoons peanut oil
1 cup pearl onions, peeled

*Directions*
Place the tofu, Worcestershire sauce, vinegar, maple syrup, shallot powder, porcini powder, and garlic powder in a ceramic dish. Let it marinate in your refrigerator for 1 hour.
Transfer the tofu to the lightly greased Air Fryer basket. Add the peanut oil and pearl onions; toss to combine.
Cook the tofu with the pearl onions in the preheated Air Fryer at 380 degrees F for 6 minutes; pause and brush with the reserved marinade; cook for a further 5 minutes.
Serve immediately. Bon appétit!

## Easy Vegan "Chicken"

*(Ready in about 20 minutes | Servings 4)*
**Per serving:** 348 Calories; 12.1g Fat; 41.5g Carbs; 21.7g Protein; 4.5g Sugars

*Ingredients*
8 ounces soy chunks
1/2 cup cornmeal
1/4 cup all-purpose flour
1 teaspoon cayenne pepper
1/2 teaspoon mustard powder
1 teaspoon celery seeds
Sea salt and ground black pepper, to taste

*Directions*
Boil the soya chunks in lots of water in a saucepan over medium-high heat. Remove from the heat and let them soak for 10 minutes.
Drain, rinse, and squeeze off the excess water.
Mix the remaining ingredients in a bowl. Roll the soy chunks over the breading mixture, pressing to adhere.
Arrange the soy chunks in the lightly greased Air Fryer basket.
Cook in the preheated Air Fryer at 390 degrees for 10 minutes, turning them over halfway through the cooking time; work in batches. Bon appétit!

## The Best Falafel Ever

*(Ready in about 20 minutes | Servings 2)*
**Per serving:** 411 Calories; 6.1g Fat; 70.2g Carbs; 21.4g Protein; 12.2g Sugars

*Ingredients*
1 cup dried chickpeas, soaked overnight
1 small-sized onion, chopped
2 cloves garlic, minced
2 tablespoons fresh cilantro leaves, chopped
1 tablespoon flour
1/2 teaspoon baking powder
1 teaspoon cumin powder
A pinch of ground cardamom
Sea salt and ground black pepper, to taste

*Directions*
Pulse all the ingredients in your food processor until the chickpeas are ground.

Form the falafel mixture into balls and place them in the lightly greased Air Fryer basket.

Cook at 380 degrees F for about 15 minutes, shaking the basket occasionally to ensure even cooking.

Serve in pita bread with toppings of your choice. Enjoy!

# Onion Rings with Spicy Ketchup

*(Ready in about 30 minutes | Servings 2)*

**Per serving:** 361 Calories; 4.5g Fat; 67.5g Carbs; 12.1g Protein; 10.5g Sugars

*Ingredients*

1 onion, sliced into rings

1/3 cup all-purpose flour

1/2 cup oat milk

1 teaspoon curry powder

1 teaspoon cayenne pepper

Salt and ground black pepper, to your liking

1/2 cup cornmeal

4 tablespoons vegan parmesan

1/4 cup spicy ketchup

*Directions*

Place the onion rings in the bowl with cold water; let them soak approximately 20 minutes; drain the onion rings and pat dry using a kitchen towel.

In a shallow bowl, mix the flour, milk, curry powder, cayenne pepper, salt, and black pepper. Mix to combine well.

Mix the cornmeal and vegan parmesan in another shallow bowl. Dip the onion rings in the flour/milk mixture; then, dredge in the cornmeal mixture.

Spritz the Air Fryer basket with cooking spray; arrange the breaded onion rings in the Air Fryer basket.

Cook in the preheated Air Fryer at 400 degrees F for 4 to 5 minutes, turning them over halfway through the cooking time. Serve with spicy ketchup. Bon appétit!

# Spicy Roasted Cashew Nuts

*(Ready in about 20 minutes | Servings 4)*

**Per serving:** 400 Calories; 35.1g Fat; 19.3g Carbs; 7.7g Protein; 5.8g Sugars

*Ingredients*

1 cup whole cashews

1 teaspoon olive oil

Salt and ground black pepper, to taste

1/2 teaspoon smoked paprika

1/2 teaspoon ancho chili powder

*Directions*

Toss all ingredients in the mixing bowl.

Line the Air Fryer basket with baking parchment. Spread out the spiced cashews in a single layer in the basket.

Roast at 350 degrees F for 6 to 8 minutes, shaking the basket once or twice. Work in batches. Enjoy!

# Barbecue Tofu with Green Beans

*(Ready in about 1 hour | Servings 3)*

**Per serving:** 316 Calories; 19.8g Fat; 20.8g Carbs; 20.1g Protein; 8.1g Sugars

*Ingredients*

12 ounces super firm tofu, pressed and cubed

1/4 cup ketchup

1 tablespoon white vinegar

1 tablespoon coconut sugar

1 tablespoon mustard

1/4 teaspoon ground black pepper

1/2 teaspoon sea salt

1/4 teaspoon smoked paprika

1/2 teaspoon freshly grated ginger

2 cloves garlic, minced

2 tablespoons olive oil
1 pound green beans

***Directions***

Toss the tofu with the ketchup, white vinegar, coconut sugar, mustard, black pepper, sea salt, paprika, ginger, garlic, and olive oil. Let it marinate for 30 minutes.

Cook at 360 degrees F for 10 minutes; turn them over and cook for 12 minutes more. Reserve.

Place the green beans in the lightly greased Air Fryer basket. Roast at 400 degrees F for 5 minutes. Bon appétit!

## Cinnamon Sugar Tortilla Chips

*(Ready in about 20 minutes | Servings 4)*
**Per serving:** 270 Calories; 14.1g Fat; 32.7g Carbs; 3.8g Protein; 7.7g Sugars

***Ingredients***

4 (10-inch) flour tortillas
1/4 cup vegan margarine, melted
1 ½ tablespoons ground cinnamon
1/4 cup caster sugar

***Directions***

Slice each tortilla into eight slices. Brush the tortilla pieces with the melted margarine.

In a mixing bowl, thoroughly combine the cinnamon and sugar. Toss the cinnamon mixture with the tortillas.

Transfer to the cooking basket and cook at 360 degrees F for 8 minutes or until lightly golden. Work in batches.

They will crisp up as they cool. Serve and enjoy!

## Tofu and Brown Rice Bake

*(Ready in about 55 minutes + marinating time| Servings 4)*

**Per serving:** 402 Calories; 14.7g Fat; 54.7g Carbs; 15.3g Protein; 8.3g Sugars

***Ingredients***

1 cup brown rice
16 ounces extra firm tofu, pressed, drained, and cut into bite-sized cubes
Marinade:
2 tablespoons sesame oil
1/2 cup tamari sauce
2 tablespoons maple syrup
1 tablespoon white vinegar
1 teaspoon hot sauce
4 tablespoons cornstarch
Salt and black pepper, to taste

***Directions***

Heat the brown rice and 2 ½ cups of water in a saucepan over high heat. Bring it to a boil; turn the stove down to simmer and cook for 35 minutes.

Place the tofu in a ceramic dish; add the remaining ingredients for the marinade and whisk to combine well. Allow it to marinate for 1 hour in your refrigerator.

Grease a baking pan with nonstick cooking spray. Add the hot rice and place the tofu on the top. Stir in the reserved marinade.

Cook at 370 degrees F for 15 minutes, checking occasionally to ensure even cooking. Enjoy!

## Healthy Mac and Cheese

*(Ready in about 30 minutes | Servings 4)*
**Per serving:** 449 Calories; 18.3g Fat; 55.5g Carbs; 14.2g Protein; 9.7g Sugars

***Ingredients***

12 ounces elbow pasta
2 garlic cloves, minced
1/3 cup vegan margarine
1/3 cup chickpea flour

3/4 cup unsweetened almond milk

2 heaping tablespoons nutritional yeast

1/2 teaspoon curry powder

1/2 teaspoon mustard powder

1/2 teaspoon celery seeds

Sea salt and white pepper, to taste

1 ½ cups pasta water

1/2 cup seasoned breadcrumbs

1 heaping tablespoon Italian parsley, roughly chopped

*Directions*

Bring a pot of salted water to a boil over high heat; turn the heat down to medium and add the elbow pasta.

Let it cook approximately 8 minutes. Drain and transfer to the lightly greased baking pan.

In a mixing dish, thoroughly combine the garlic, margarine, chickpea flour, milk, nutritional yeast, and spices. Add the pasta water and mix to combine well.

Pour the milk mixture into the baking pan; gently stir to combine. Top with the seasoned breadcrumbs.

Bake in the preheated Air Fryer at 360 degrees F for 15 minutes. Serve garnished with fresh parsley leaves. Bon appétit!

# Cauliflower, Broccoli and Chickpea Salad

*(Ready in about 20 minutes + chilling time | Servings 4)*

**Per serving:** 263 Calories; 15.8g Fat; 24.8g Carbs; 9.4g Protein; 6.1g Sugars

*Ingredients*

1/2 pound cauliflower florets

1/2 pound broccoli florets

Sea salt, to taste

1/2 teaspoon red pepper flakes

2 tablespoons soy sauce

2 tablespoons cider vinegar

1 teaspoon Dijon mustard

2 tablespoons extra-virgin olive oil

1 cup canned or cooked chickpeas, drained

1 avocado, pitted, peeled and sliced

1 small sized onion, peeled and sliced

1 garlic clove, minced

2 cups arugula

2 tablespoons sesame seeds, lightly toasted

*Directions*

Start by preheating your Air Fryer to 400 degrees F.

Brush the cauliflower and broccoli florets with cooking spray.

Cook for 12 minutes, shaking the cooking basket halfway through the cooking time. Season with salt and red pepper.

In a mixing dish, whisk the soy sauce, cider vinegar, Dijon mustard, and olive oil. Dress the salad. Add the chickpeas, avocado, onion, garlic, and arugula. Top with sesame seeds.

Bon appétit!

# Butternut Squash Chili

*(Ready in about 35 minutes | Servings 4)*

**Per serving:** 295 Calories; 18.9g Fat; 29.3g Carbs; 7g Protein; 4.6g Sugars

*Ingredients*

2 tablespoons canola oil

1 cup leeks, chopped

2 garlic cloves, crushed

2 ripe tomatoes, pureed

2 chipotle peppers in adobo, chopped

1 teaspoon ground cumin

1 teaspoon chili powder

Kosher salt and ground black pepper, to your liking

1 cup vegetable broth

1 pound butternut squash, peeled and diced into 1/2-inch chunks

16 ounces canned kidney beans, drained and rinsed

1 avocado, pitted, peeled and diced

*Directions*

Start by preheating your Air Fryer to 365 degrees F.

Heat the oil in a baking pan until sizzling. Then, sauté the leeks and garlic in the baking pan. Cook for 4 to 6 minutes.

Now, add the tomatoes, chipotle peppers, cumin, chili powder, salt, pepper, and vegetable broth. Cook for 15 minutes, stirring every 5 minutes.

Stir in the the butternut squash and canned beans; let it cook for a further 8 minutes, stirring halfway through the cooking time.

Serve in individual bowls, garnished with the avocado. Enjoy!

## Ultimate Vegan Calzone

*(Ready in about 25 minutes | Servings 1)*

**Per serving:** 535 Calories; 14g Fat; 88.2g Carbs; 16g Protein; 19g Sugars

*Ingredients*

1 teaspoon olive oil

1/2 small onion, chopped

2 sweet peppers, seeded and sliced

Sea salt, to taste

1/4 teaspoon ground black pepper

1/4 teaspoon dried oregano

4 ounces prepared Italian pizza dough

1/4 cup marinara sauce

2 ounces plant-based cheese Mozzarella-style, shredded

*Directions*

Heat the olive oil in a nonstick skillet. Once hot, cook the onion and peppers until tender and fragrant, about 5 minutes. Add salt, black pepper, and oregano.

Sprinkle some flour on a kitchen counter and roll out the pizza dough.

Spoon the marinara sauce over half of the dough; add the sautéed mixture and sprinkle with the vegan cheese. Now, gently fold over the dough to create a pocket; make sure to seal the edges.

Use a fork to poke the dough in a few spots. Add a few drizzles of olive oil and place in the lightly greased cooking basket.

Bake in the preheated Air Fryer at 330 degrees F for 12 minutes, turning the calzones over halfway through the cooking time. Bon appétit!

## Mediterranean-Style Potato Chips with Vegveeta Dip

*(Ready in about 1 hour | Servings 4)*

**Per serving:** 244 Calories; 18g Fat; 19.4g Carbs; 4g Protein; 1.7g Sugars

*Ingredients*

1 large potato, cut into 1/8 inch thick slices

1 tablespoon olive oil

Sea salt, to taste

1/2 teaspoon red pepper flakes, crushed

1 teaspoon fresh rosemary

1/2 teaspoon fresh sage

1/2 teaspoon fresh basil

Dipping Sauce:

1/3 cup raw cashews

1 tablespoon tahini

1 ½ tablespoons olive oil

1/4 cup raw almonds

1/4 teaspoon prepared yellow mustard

*Directions*

Soak the potatoes in a large bowl of cold water for 20 to 30 minutes. Drain the potatoes and pat them dry with a kitchen towel.

Toss with olive oil and seasonings.

Place in the lightly greased cooking basket and cook at 380 degrees F for 30 minutes. Work in batches.

Meanwhile, puree the sauce ingredients in your food processor until smooth. Serve the potato chips with the Vegveeta sauce for dipping. Bon appétit!

## Sunday Potato Fritters

*(Ready in about 30 minutes | Servings 3)*

**Per serving:** 367 Calories; 8.9g Fat; 60.6g Carbs; 12.8g Protein; 7.5g Sugars

*Ingredients*

1 tablespoon olive oil
1/2 pound potatoes, peeled and cut into chunks
1/2 cup cashew cream
1/2 cup chickpea flour
1/2 teaspoon baking powder
1/2 onion, chopped
1 garlic clove, minced
Sea salt and ground black pepper, to your liking
1 cup tortilla chips, crushed

*Directions*

Start by preheating your Air Fryer to 400 degrees F.

Drizzle the olive oil all over the potatoes. Place the potatoes in the Air Fryer basket and cook approximately 15 minutes, shaking the basket periodically.

Lightly crush the potatoes to split; mash the potatoes and combine with the other ingredients. Form the potato mixture into patties.

Bake in the preheated Air Fryer at 380 degrees F for 14 minutes, flipping them halfway through the cooking time to ensure even cooking. Bon appétit!

## Paprika Brussels Sprout Chips

*(Ready in about 20 minutes | Servings 2)*

**Per serving:** 64 Calories; 2.6g Fat; 9.1g Carbs; 3.3g Protein; 2.2g Sugars

*Ingredients*

10 Brussels sprouts
1 teaspoon canola oil
1 teaspoon coarse sea salt
1 teaspoon paprika

*Directions*

Toss all ingredients in the lightly greased Air Fryer basket.

Bake at 380 degrees F for 15 minutes, shaking the basket halfway through the cooking time to ensure even cooking.

Serve and enjoy!

## Vegetable Kabobs with Simple Peanut Sauce

*(Ready in about 30 minutes | Servings 4)*

**Per serving:** 323 Calories; 8.8g Fat; 56g Carbs; 7.6g Protein; 11.5g Sugars

*Ingredients*

8 whole baby potatoes, diced into 1-inch pieces
2 bell peppers, diced into 1-inch pieces
8 pearl onions, halved
8 small button mushrooms, cleaned
2 tablespoons extra-virgin olive oil
Sea salt and ground black pepper, to taste
1 teaspoon red pepper flakes, crushed
1 teaspoon dried rosemary, crushed
1/3 teaspoon granulated garlic

Peanut Sauce:

2 tablespoons peanut butter

1 tablespoon balsamic vinegar

1 tablespoon soy sauce

1/2 teaspoon garlic salt

*Directions*

Soak the wooden skewers in water for 15 minutes. Thread the vegetables on skewers; drizzle the olive oil all over the vegetable skewers; sprinkle with spices.

Cook in the preheated Air Fryer at 400 degrees F for 13 minutes.

Meanwhile, in a small dish, whisk the peanut butter with the balsamic vinegar, soy sauce, and garlic salt. Serve your kabobs with the peanut sauce on the side. Enjoy!

# Baked Spicy Tortilla Chips

*(Ready in about 20 minutes | Servings 3)*

**Per serving:** 189 Calories; 5.1g Fat; 30.7g Carbs; 4.7g Protein; 2g Sugars

*Ingredients*

6 (6-inch) corn tortillas

1 teaspoon canola oil

1 teaspoon salt

1/4 teaspoon ground white pepper

1/2 teaspoon ground cumin

1/2 teaspoon ancho chili powder

*Directions*

Slice the tortillas into quarters. Brush the tortilla pieces with the canola oil until well coated.

Toss with the spices and transfer to the Air Fryer basket.

Bake at 360 degrees F for 8 minutes or until lightly golden. Work in batches. Bon appétit!

# Barbecue Roasted Almonds

*(Ready in about 20 minutes | Servings 6)*

**Per serving:** 340 Calories; 30.1g Fat; 11.5g Carbs; 11.3g Protein; 2.3g Sugars

*Ingredients*

1 ½ cups raw almonds

Sea salt and ground black pepper, to taste

1/4 teaspoon garlic powder

1/4 teaspoon mustard powder

1/2 teaspoon cumin powder

1/4 teaspoon smoked paprika

1 tablespoon olive oil

*Directions*

Toss all ingredients in a mixing bowl.

Line the Air Fryer basket with baking parchment. Spread out the coated almonds in a single layer in the basket.

Roast at 350 degrees F for 6 to 8 minutes, shaking the basket once or twice. Work in batches. Enjoy!

# DESSERTS

## Grilled Banana Boats

*(Ready in about 15 minutes | Servings 3)*
**Per serving:** 269 Calories; 5.9g Fat; 47.9g Carbs; 2.6g Protein; 28.3g Sugars

*Ingredients*

3 large bananas

1 tablespoon ginger snaps

2 tablespoons mini chocolate chips

3 tablespoons mini marshmallows

3 tablespoons crushed vanilla wafers

*Directions*

In the peel, slice your banana lengthwise; make sure not to slice all the way through the banana. Divide the remaining ingredients between the banana pockets.

Place in the Air Fryer grill pan. Cook at 395 degrees F for 7 minutes.

Let the banana boats cool for 5 to 6 minutes, and then eat with a spoon. Bon appétit!

## Chocolate Birthday Cake

*(Ready in about 35 minutes + chilling time | Servings 6)*
**Per serving:** 689 Calories; 43.4g Fat; 76.1g Carbs; 6.5g Protein; 55.6g Sugars

*Ingredients*

2 eggs, beaten

2/3 cup sour cream

1 cup flour

1/2 cup sugar

1/4 cup honey

1/3 cup coconut oil, softened

1/4 cup cocoa powder

2 tablespoons chocolate chips

1 ½ teaspoons baking powder

1 teaspoon vanilla extract

1/2 teaspoon pure rum extract

Chocolate Frosting:

1/2 cup butter, softened

1/4 cup cocoa powder

2 cups powdered sugar

2 tablespoons milk

*Directions*

Mix all ingredients for the chocolate cake with a hand mixer on low speed. Scrape the batter into a cake pan.

Bake at 330 degrees F for 25 to 30 minutes. Transfer the cake to a wire rack

Meanwhile, whip the butter and cocoa until smooth. Stir in the powdered sugar. Slowly and gradually, pour in the milk until your frosting reaches desired consistency.

Whip until smooth and fluffy; then, frost the cooled cake. Place in your refrigerator for a couple of hours. Serve well chilled.

## Favorite New York Cheesecake

*(Ready in about 40 minutes + chilling time | Servings 8)*
**Per serving:** 477 Calories; 30.2g Fat; 39.5g Carbs; 12.8g Protein; 32.9g Sugars

*Ingredients*

1 ½ cups digestive biscuits crumbs

2 ounces white sugar

1 ounce demerara sugar

1/2 stick butter, melted

32 ounces full-fat cream cheese

1/2 cup heavy cream

1 ¼ cups caster sugar

3 eggs, at room temperature

1 tablespoon vanilla essence

1 teaspoon grated lemon zest

*Directions*

Coat the sides and bottom of a baking pan with a little flour.

In a mixing bowl, combine the digestive biscuits, white sugar, and demerara sugar. Add the melted butter and mix until your mixture looks like breadcrumbs.

Press the mixture into the bottom of the prepared pan to form an even layer. Bake at 330 degrees F for 7 minutes until golden brown. Allow it to cool completely on a wire rack.

Meanwhile, in a mixer fitted with the paddle attachment, prepare the filling by mixing the soft cheese, heavy cream, and caster sugar; beat until creamy and fluffy.

Crack the eggs into the mixing bowl, one at a time; add the vanilla and lemon zest and continue to mix until fully combined.

Pour the prepared topping over the cooled crust and spread evenly.

Bake in the preheated Air Fryer at 330 degrees F for 25 to 30 minutes; leave it in the Air Fryer to keep warm for another 30 minutes.

Cover your cheesecake with plastic wrap. Place in your refrigerator and allow it to cool at least 6 hours or overnight. Serve well chilled.

# English-Style Scones with Raisins

*(Ready in about 20 minutes | Servings 6)*

**Per serving:** 317 Calories; 18.9g Fat; 29.5g Carbs; 6.9g Protein; 5.2g Sugars

*Ingredients*

1 ½ cups all-purpose flour

1/4 cup brown sugar

1 teaspoon baking powder

1/4 teaspoon sea salt

1/4 teaspoon ground cloves

1/2 teaspoon ground cardamom

1 teaspoon ground cinnamon

1/2 cup raisins

6 tablespoons butter, cooled and sliced

1/2 cup double cream

2 eggs, lightly whisked

1/2 teaspoon vanilla essence

*Directions*

In a mixing bowl, thoroughly combine the flour, sugar, baking powder, salt, cloves, cardamom cinnamon, and raisins. Mix until everything is combined well.

Add the butter and mix again.

In another mixing bowl, combine the double cream with the eggs and vanilla; beat until creamy and smooth.

Stir the wet ingredients into the dry mixture. Roll your dough out into a circle and cut into wedges. Bake in the preheated Air Fryer at 360 degrees for 11 minutes, rotating the pan halfway through the cooking time. Bon appétit!

# Baked Peaches with Oatmeal Pecan Streusel

*(Ready in about 20 minutes | Servings 3)*

**Per serving:** 247 Calories; 14.1g Fat; 28.8g Carbs; 5.9g Protein; 23.1g Sugars

*Ingredients*

2 tablespoons old-fashioned rolled oats

3 tablespoons golden caster sugar

1/2 teaspoon ground cinnamon

1 egg

2 tablespoons cold salted butter, cut into pieces

3 tablespoons pecans, chopped

3 large ripe freestone peaches, halved and pitted

*Directions*

Mix the rolled oats, sugar, cinnamon, egg, and butter until well combined.

Add a big spoonful of prepared topping to the center of each peach. Pour 1/2 cup of water into an Air Fryer safe dish. Place the peaches in the dish.

Top the peaches with the roughly chopped pecans. Bake at 340 degrees F for 17 minutes. Serve at room temperature. Bon appétit!

## Red Velvet Pancakes

*(Ready in about 35 minutes | Servings 3)*

**Per serving:** 392 Calories; 17.8g Fat; 50g Carbs; 7.8g Protein; 33.2g Sugars

*Ingredients*

1/2 cup flour

1 teaspoon baking powder

1/4 teaspoon salt

2 tablespoons white sugar

1/2 teaspoon cinnamon

1 teaspoon red paste food color

1 egg

1/2 cup milk

1 teaspoon vanilla

Topping:

2 ounces cream cheese, softened

2 tablespoons butter, softened

3/4 cup powdered sugar

*Directions*

Mix the flour, baking powder, salt, sugar, cinnamon, red paste food color in a large bowl.

Gradually add the egg and milk, whisking continuously, until well combined. Let it stand for 20 minutes.

Spritz the Air Fryer baking pan with cooking spray. Pour the batter into the pan using a measuring cup.

Cook at 230 degrees F for 4 to 5 minutes or until golden brown. Repeat with the remaining batter. Meanwhile, make your topping by mixing the ingredients until creamy and fluffy. Decorate your pancakes with topping. Bon appétit!

## Spanish-Style Doughnut Tejeringos

*(Ready in about 20 minutes | Servings 4)*

**Per serving:** 311 Calories; 22.3g Fat; 20.5g Carbs; 7.1g Protein; 2.4g Sugars

*Ingredients*

3/4 cup water

1 tablespoon sugar

1/4 teaspoon sea salt

1/4 teaspoon grated nutmeg

1/4 teaspoon ground cloves

6 tablespoons butter

3/4 cup all-purpose flour

2 eggs

*Directions*

To make the dough, boil the water in a pan over medium-high heat; now, add the sugar, salt, nutmeg, and cloves; cook until dissolved.

Add the butter and turn the heat to low. Gradually stir in the flour, whisking continuously, until the mixture forms a ball.

Remove from the heat; fold in the eggs one at a time, stirring to combine well.

Pour the mixture into a piping bag with a large star tip. Squeeze 4-inch strips of dough into the greased Air Fryer pan.

Cook at 410 degrees F for 6 minutes, working in batches. Bon appétit!

# Baked Fruit Compote with Coconut Chips

*(Ready in about 25 minutes | Servings 6)*
**Per serving:** 215 Calories; 7.5g Fat; 38.2g Carbs; 1.2g Protein; 29.6g Sugars

*Ingredients*

1 tablespoon butter

8 ounces canned apricot halves, drained

8 ounces canned pear halves, drained

16 ounces pineapple slices, undrained

1/3 cup packed brown sugar

1/4 teaspoon grated nutmeg

1/4 teaspoon ground cloves

1/2 teaspoon ground cinnamon

1 teaspoon pure vanilla extract

1/2 cup coconut chips

*Directions*

Start by preheating your Air Fryer to 330 degrees F. Grease a baking pan with butter.

Place all ingredients, except for the coconut chips, in a baking pan. Bake in the preheated Air Fryer for 20 minutes.

Serve in individual bowls, garnished with coconut chips. Bon appétit!

# Summer Peach Crisp

*(Ready in about 40 minutes | Servings 4)*
**Per serving:** 330 Calories; 16.6g Fat; 48.2g Carbs; 4.2g Protein; 30.8g Sugars

*Ingredients*

2 cups fresh peaches, pitted and sliced

1/4 cup cornmeal

1/4 cup brown sugar

1 teaspoon pure vanilla extract

1/2 teaspoon ground cinnamon

A pinch of fine sea salt

1 stick cold butter

1/2 cup rolled oats

*Directions*

Toss the sliced peaches with the cornmeal, brown sugar, vanilla extract, cinnamon, and sea salt. Place in a baking pan coated with cooking spray. In a mixing dish, thoroughly combine the cold butter and rolled oats. Sprinkle the mixture over each peach.

Bake in the preheated Air Fryer at 330 degrees F for 35 minutes. Bon appétit!

# Greek-Style Griddle Cakes

*(Ready in about 15 minutes | Servings 4)*
**Per serving:** 276 Calories; 8.5g Fat; 40.2g Carbs; 10.4g Protein; 19.4g Sugars

*Ingredients*

3/4 cup self-raising flour

1/4 teaspoon fine sea salt

2 tablespoons sugar

1/2 cup milk

2 eggs, lightly beaten

1 tablespoon butter

Topping:

1 cup Greek-style yogurt

1 banana, mashed

2 tablespoons honey

*Directions*

Mix the flour, salt, and sugar in a bowl. Then, stir in the milk, eggs, and butter. Mix until smooth and uniform.

Drop tablespoons of the batter into the Air Fryer pan.

Cook at 300 degrees F for 4 to 5 minutes or until bubbles form on top of the griddle cakes. Repeat with the remaining batter.

Meanwhile, mix all ingredients for the topping. Place in your refrigerator until ready to serve. Serve the griddle cakes with the chilled topping. Enjoy!

# Nana's Famous Apple Fritters

*(Ready in about 20 minutes | Servings 4)*
**Per serving:** 280 Calories; 5.7g Fat; 51.1g Carbs;
7.4g Protein; 30.8g Sugars

### Ingredients

2/3 cup all-purpose flour
3 tablespoons granulated sugar
A pinch of sea salt
A pinch of freshly grated nutmeg
1 teaspoon baking powder
2 eggs, whisked
1/4 cup milk
2 apples, peeled, cored and diced
1/2 cup powdered sugar

### Directions

Mix the flour, sugar, salt, nutmeg and baking powder.

In a separate bowl whisk the eggs with the milk; add this wet mixture into the dry ingredients; mix to combine well.

Add the apple pieces and mix again.

Cook in the preheated Air Fryer at 370 degrees for 3 minutes, flipping them halfway through the cooking time. Repeat with the remaining batter. Dust with powdered sugar and serve at room temperature. Bon appétit!

# Authentic Indian Gulgulas

*(Ready in about 20 minutes | Servings 3)*
**Per serving:** 252 Calories; 4.9g Fat; 43.8g Carbs;
7.9g Protein; 15.4g Sugars

### Ingredients

1 banana, mashed
1/4 cup sugar
1 egg
1/2 teaspoon vanilla essence
1/4 teaspoon ground cardamom
1/4 teaspoon cinnamon
1/2 milk
3/4 cup all-purpose flour
1 teaspoon baking powder

### Directions

In a mixing bowl, whisk the mashed banana with the sugar and egg; add the vanilla, cardamom, and cinnamon and mix to combine well.

Gradually pour in the milk and mix again. Stir in the flour and baking powder. Mix until everything is well incorporated.

Drop a spoonful of batter onto the greased Air Fryer pan. Cook in the preheated Air Fryer at 360 degrees F for 5 minutes, flipping them halfway through the cooking time.

Repeat with the remaining batter and serve warm. Enjoy!

# Coconut Pancake Cups

*(Ready in about 30 minutes | Servings 4)*
**Per serving:** 274 Calories; 17.3g Fat; 21.6g Carbs;
7.7g Protein; 1.5g Sugars

### Ingredients

1/2 cup flour
1/3 cup coconut milk
2 eggs
1 tablespoon coconut oil, melted
1 teaspoon vanilla
A pinch of ground cardamom
1/2 cup coconut chips

### Directions

Mix the flour, coconut milk, eggs, coconut oil, vanilla, and cardamom in a large bowl.

Let it stand for 20 minutes. Spoon the batter into a greased muffin tin.

Cook at 230 degrees F for 4 to 5 minutes or until golden brown. Repeat with the remaining batter. Decorate your pancakes with coconut chips. Bon appétit!

# Salted Caramel Cheesecake

*(Ready in about 1 hour + chilling time | Servings 10)*

**Per serving:** 501 Calories; 36.3g Fat; 35.6g Carbs; 9.1g Protein; 24.2g Sugars

### Ingredients

1 cup granulated sugar

1/3 cup water

3/4 cup heavy cream

2 tablespoons butter

1 teaspoon vanilla extract

1/2 teaspoon coarse sea salt

Crust:

1 ½ cups graham cracker crumbs

1/3 cup salted butter, melted

2 tablespoons brown sugar

Topping:

20 ounces cream cheese, softened

1 cup sour cream

1 cup granulated sugar

1 teaspoon vanilla essence

1/4 teaspoon ground star anise

3 eggs

### Directions

To make the caramel sauce, cook the sugar in a saucepan over medium heat; shake it to form a flat layer.

Add the water and cook until the sugar dissolves. Raise the heat to medium-high, and continue to cook your caramel for a further 10 minutes until it turns amber colored.

Turn the heat off; immediately stir in the heavy cream, butter, vanilla extract, and salt. Stir to combine well.

Let the salted caramel sauce cool to room temperature.

Beat all ingredients for the crust in a mixing bowl. Press the mixture into the bottom of a lightly greased baking pan.

Bake at 350 degrees F for 18 minutes. Place it in your freezer for 20 minutes.

Then, make the cheesecake topping by mixing the remaining ingredients. Pour the prepared topping over the cooled crust and spread evenly. Bake in the preheated Air Fryer at 330 degrees F for 25 to 30 minutes; leave it in the Air Fryer to keep warm for another 30 minutes.

Refrigerate your cheesecake until completely cool and firm or overnight. Prior to serving, pour the salted caramel sauce over the cheesecake. Bon appétit!

# Banana Crepes with Apple Topping

*(Ready in about 40 minutes | Servings 2)*

**Per serving:** 367 Calories; 12.1g Fat; 57.7g Carbs; 10.2g Protein; 43.6g Sugars

### Ingredients

Banana Crepes:

1 large banana, mashed

2 eggs, beaten

1/4 teaspoon baking powder

1 shot dark rum

1/2 teaspoon vanilla extract

1 teaspoon butter, melted

2 tablespoons brown sugar

Topping:

2 apples, peeled, cored, and chopped

2 tablespoons sugar

1/2 teaspoon cinnamon

3 tablespoons water

### Directions

Mix all ingredients for the banana crepes until creamy and fluffy. Let it stand for 15 to 20 minutes.

Spritz the Air Fryer baking pan with cooking spray. Pour the batter into the pan using a measuring cup.

Cook at 230 degrees F for 4 to 5 minutes or until golden brown. Repeat with the remaining batter. To make the pancake topping, place all ingredients in a heavy-bottomed skillet over medium heat. Cook for 10 minutes, stirring occasionally. Spoon on top of the banana crepes and enjoy!

## Apricot and Walnut Crumble

*(Ready in about 40 minutes | Servings 8)*

**Per serving:** 404 Calories; 16.4g Fat; 69.2g Carbs; 5.6g Protein; 52.1g Sugars

*Ingredients*

2 pounds apricots, pitted and sliced

1 cup brown sugar

2 tablespoons cornstarch

Topping:

1 ½ cups old-fashioned rolled oats

1/2 cup brown sugar

2 tablespoons agave nectar

1 teaspoon crystallized ginger

1/2 teaspoon ground cardamom

A pinch of salt

1 stick butter, cut into pieces

1/2 cup walnuts, chopped

1/2 cup dried cranberries

*Directions*

Toss the sliced apricots with the brown sugar and cornstarch. Place in a baking pan lightly greased with nonstick cooking spray.

In a mixing dish, thoroughly combine all the topping ingredients. Sprinkle the topping ingredients over the apricot layer.

Bake in the preheated Air Fryer at 330 degrees F for 35 minutes. Bon appétit!

## Butter Rum Cookies with Walnuts

*(Ready in about 35 minutes | Servings 6)*

**Per serving:** 364 Calories; 26.9g Fat; 26.3g Carbs; 5.9g Protein; 8.7g Sugars

*Ingredients*

1 cup all-purpose flour

1/2 teaspoon baking powder

1/4 teaspoon fine sea salt

1 stick butter, unsalted and softened

1/2 cup sugar

1 egg

1/2 teaspoon vanilla

1 teaspoon butter rum flavoring

3 ounces walnuts, finely chopped

*Directions*

Begin by preheating the Air Fryer to 360 degrees F.

In a mixing dish, thoroughly combine the flour with baking powder and salt.

Beat the butter and sugar with a hand mixer until pale and fluffy; add the whisked egg, vanilla, and butter rum flavoring; mix again to combine well. Now, stir in the dry ingredients.

Fold in the chopped walnuts and mix to combine. Divide the mixture into small balls; flatten each ball with a fork and transfer them to a foil-lined baking pan.

Bake in the preheated Air Fryer for 14 minutes. Work in a few batches and transfer to wire racks to cool completely. Bon appétit!

## Classic Butter Cake

*(Ready in about 35 minutes | Servings 8)*

**Per serving:** 244 Calories; 14.2g Fat; 25.1g Carbs; 4.2g Protein; 12.8g Sugars

*Ingredients*

1 stick butter, at room temperature

1 cup sugar

2 eggs

1 cup all-purpose flour

1 teaspoon baking powder

1/2 teaspoon baking soda

1/4 teaspoon salt

A pinch of freshly grated nutmeg

A pinch of ground star anise

1/4 cup buttermilk

1 teaspoon vanilla essence

### Directions

Begin by preheating your Air Fryer to 320 degrees F. Spritz the bottom and sides of a baking pan with cooking spray.

Beat the butter and sugar with a hand mixer until creamy. Then, fold in the eggs, one at a time, and mix well until fluffy.

Stir in the flour along with the remaining ingredients. Mix to combine well. Scrape the batter into the prepared baking pan.

Bake for 15 minutes; rotate the pan and bake an additional 15 minutes, until the top of the cake springs back when gently pressed with your fingers. Bon appétit!

## Pecan Fudge Brownies

*(Ready in about 30 minutes | Servings 6)*
**Per serving:** 341 Calories; 23.5g Fat; 31.3g Carbs; 4.2g Protein; 19.2g Sugars

### Ingredients

1/2 cup butter, melted

1/2 cup sugar

1 teaspoon vanilla essence

1 egg

1/2 cup flour

1/2 teaspoon baking powder

1/4 cup cocoa powder

1/2 teaspoon ground cinnamon

1/4 teaspoon fine sea salt

1 ounce semisweet chocolate, coarsely chopped

1/4 cup pecans, finely chopped

### Directions

Start by preheating your Air Fryer to 350 degrees F. Now, lightly grease six silicone molds.

In a mixing dish, beat the melted butter with the sugar until fluffy. Next, stir in the vanilla and egg and beat again.

After that, add the flour, baking powder, cocoa powder, cinnamon, and salt. Mix until everything is well combined.

Fold in the chocolate and pecans; mix to combine. Bake in the preheated Air Fryer for 20 to 22 minutes. Enjoy!

## Fried Honey Banana

*(Ready in about 20 minutes | Servings 2)*
**Per serving:** 363 Calories; 14.3g Fat; 61.1g Carbs; 3.7g Protein; 33.3g Sugars

### Ingredients

2 ripe bananas, peeled and sliced

2 tablespoons honey

3 tablespoons rice flour

3 tablespoons desiccated coconut

A pinch of fine sea salt

1/2 teaspoon baking powder

1/4 teaspoon cardamom powder

### Directions

Preheat the Air Fryer to 390 degrees F.

Drizzle honey over the banana slices.

In a mixing dish, thoroughly combine the rice flour, coconut, salt, baking powder, and cardamom powder. Roll each slice of banana over the flour mixture.

Bake in the preheated Air Fryer approximately 13 minutes, flipping them halfway through the cooking time. Bon appétit!

# Pop Tarts with Homemade Strawberry Jam

*(Ready in about 45 minutes | Servings 8)*
**Per serving:** 173 Calories; 8.9g Fat; 20.1g Carbs; 3.6g Protein; 7.7g Sugars

*Ingredients*
1 cup strawberries, sliced
1 tablespoon fresh lemon juice
1 teaspoon maple syrup
2 tablespoons chia seeds
1 (14-ounce) box refrigerated pie crust
1 egg, whisked with 1 tablespoon of water (egg wash)
1/2 cup powdered sugar

*Directions*
In a saucepan, heat the strawberries until they start to get syrupy. Mash them and add the lemon juice and maple syrup.
Remove from the heat and stir in the chia seeds. Let it stand for 30 minutes or until it thickens up. Unroll the pie crusts and cut them into small rectangles. Spoon the strawberry jam in the center of a rectangle; top with another piece of crust.
Repeat until you run out of ingredients. Line the Air Fryer basket with parchment paper.
Brush the pop tarts with the egg wash and bake at 400 degrees F for 6 minutes or until slightly brown. Work in batches and transfer to cooling racks.
Dust with powdered sugar and enjoy!

# Fall Harvest Apple Cinnamon Buns

*(Ready in about 1 hour 20 minutes | Servings 6)*
**Per serving:** 430 Calories; 16.3g Fat; 63.1g Carbs; 8g Protein; 25g Sugars

*Ingredients*
1/2 cup milk
1/2 cup granulated sugar
1 tablespoon yeast
1/2 stick butter, at room temperature
1 egg, at room temperature
1/4 teaspoon salt
2 ¼ cups all-purpose flour
Filling:
3 tablespoons butter, at room temperature
1/4 cup brown sugar
1/2 teaspoon ground cardamom
1/2 teaspoon ground cloves
1 teaspoon ground cinnamon
1 apple, peeled, cored, and chopped
1/2 cup powdered sugar

*Directions*
Heat the milk in a microwave safe bowl and transfer the warm milk to the bowl of a stand electric mixer. Add the granulated sugar and yeast, and mix to combine well. Cover and let sit until the yeast is foamy.
Then, beat the butter on low speed. Fold in the the egg and mix again. Add the salt and flour. Mix on medium speed until a soft dough forms.
Knead the dough on a lightly floured surface. Cover it loosely and let sit in a warm place about 1 hour or until doubled in size. Then, spritz the bottom and sides of a baking pan with cooking oil (butter flavored).
Roll your dough out into a rectangle.

Spread 3 tablespoons of butter all over the dough. In a mixing dish, combine the brown sugar, cardamom, cloves, and cinnamon; sprinkle evenly over the dough.

Top with the chopped apples. Then, roll up your dough to form a log. Cut into 6 equal rolls and place them in the parchment-lined Air Fryer basket.

Bake at 350 degrees for 12 minutes, turning them halfway through the cooking time. Dust with powdered sugar. Bon appétit!

# Pear Fritters with Cinnamon and Ginger

*(Ready in about 20 minutes | Servings 4)*

**Per serving:** 333 Calories; 9.5g Fat; 52.2g Carbs; 10.5g Protein; 10.9g Sugars

*Ingredients*

2 pears, peeled, cored and sliced

1 tablespoon coconut oil, melted

1 ½ cups all-purpose flour

1 teaspoon baking powder

A pinch of fine sea salt

A pinch of freshly grated nutmeg

1/2 teaspoon ginger

1 teaspoon cinnamon

2 eggs

4 tablespoons milk

*Directions*

Mix all ingredients, except for the pears, in a shallow bowl. Dip each slice of the pears in the batter until well coated.

Cook in the preheated Air Fryer at 360 degrees for 4 minutes, flipping them halfway through the cooking time. Repeat with the remaining ingredients.

Dust with powdered sugar if desired. Bon appétit!

# Old-Fashioned Plum Dumplings

*(Ready in about 40 minutes | Servings 4)*

**Per serving:** 395 Calories; 19.2g Fat; 54.5g Carbs; 4.1g Protein; 32.7g Sugars

*Ingredients*

1 (14-ounce) box pie crusts

2 cups plums, pitted

2 tablespoons granulated sugar

2 tablespoons coconut oil

1/4 teaspoon ground cardamom

1/2 teaspoon ground cinnamon

1 egg white, slightly beaten

*Directions*

Place the pie crust on a work surface. Roll into a circle and cut into quarters.

Place 1 plum on each crust piece. Add the sugar, coconut oil, cardamom, and cinnamon. Roll up the sides into a circular shape around the plums. Repeat with the remaining ingredients. Brush the edges with the egg white. Place in the lightly greased Air Fryer basket.

Bake in the preheated Air Fryer at 360 degrees F for 20 minutes, flipping them halfway through the cooking time. Work in two batches, decorate and serve at room temperature. Bon appétit!

# Almond Chocolate Cupcakes

*(Ready in about 20 minutes | Servings 6)*

**Per serving:** 288 Calories; 14.7g Fat; 35.1g Carbs; 5.1g Protein; 20g Sugars

*Ingredients*

3/4 cup self-raising flour

1 cup powdered sugar

1/4 teaspoon salt

1/4 teaspoon nutmeg, preferably freshly grated

1 tablespoon cocoa powder

2 ounces butter, softened

1 egg, whisked

2 tablespoons almond milk

1/2 teaspoon vanilla extract

1 ½ ounces dark chocolate chunks

1/2 cup almonds, chopped

*Directions*

In a mixing bowl, combine the flour, sugar, salt, nutmeg, and cocoa powder. Mix to combine well. In another mixing bowl, whisk the butter, egg, almond milk, and vanilla.

Now, add the wet egg mixture to the dry ingredients. Then, carefully fold in the chocolate chunks and almonds; gently stir to combine.

Scrape the batter mixture into muffin cups. Bake your cupcakes at 350 degrees F for 12 minutes until a toothpick comes out clean.

Decorate with chocolate sprinkles if desired. Serve and enjoy!

# White Chocolate Rum Molten Cake

*(Ready in about 20 minutes | Servings 4)*

**Per serving:** 336 Calories; 19.5g Fat; 34.5g Carbs; 6.1g Protein; 23.1g Sugars

*Ingredients*

2 ½ ounces butter, at room temperature

3 ounces white chocolate

2 eggs, beaten

1/2 cup powdered sugar

1/3 cup self-rising flour

1 teaspoon rum extract

1 teaspoon vanilla extract

*Directions*

Begin by preheating your Air Fryer to 370 degrees F. Spritz the sides and bottom of four ramekins with cooking spray.

Melt the butter and white chocolate in a microwave-safe bowl. Mix the eggs and sugar until frothy.

Pour the butter/chocolate mixture into the egg mixture. Stir in the flour, rum extract, and vanilla extract. Mix until everything is well incorporated. Scrape the batter into the prepared ramekins. Bake in the preheated Air Fryer for 9 to 11 minutes.

Let stand for 2 to 3 minutes. Invert on a plate while warm and serve. Bon appétit!

# Summer Fruit Pie with Cinnamon Streusel

*(Ready in about 40 minutes | Servings 4)*

**Per serving:** 582 Calories; 23.1g Fat; 86.5g Carbs; 8.5g Protein; 31.6g Sugars

*Ingredients*

1 (14-ounce) box pie crusts

Filling:

1/3 cup caster sugar

1/3 cup all-purpose flour

1/4 teaspoon ground cardamom

1/2 teaspoon ground cinnamon

1 teaspoon pure vanilla extract

2 cups apricots, pitted and sliced peeled

2 cups peaches, pitted and sliced peeled

Streusel:

1 cup all-purpose flour

1/2 cup brown sugar

1 teaspoon ground cinnamon

1/3 cup cold salted butter

*Directions*

Place the pie crust in a lightly greased pie plate. In a mixing bowl, thoroughly combine the caster sugar, 1/3 cup of flour, cardamom, cinnamon, and vanilla extract. Add the apricots and peaches and mix until coated. Spoon into the prepared pie crust.

Make the streusel by mixing 1 cup of flour, brown sugar, and cinnamon. Cut in the cold butter and continue to mix until the mixture looks like coarse crumbs. Sprinkle over the filling. Bake at 350 degrees F for 35 minutes or until topping is golden brown. Bon appétit!

# Mom's Orange Rolls

*(Ready in about 1 hour 20 minutes | Servings 6)*

**Per serving:** 365 Calories; 14.1g Fat; 51.9g Carbs; 7.3g Protein; 19.1g Sugars

*Ingredients*

1/2 cup milk

1/4 cup granulated sugar

1 tablespoon yeast

1/2 stick butter, at room temperature

1 egg, at room temperature

1/4 teaspoon salt

2 cups all-purpose flour

2 tablespoons fresh orange juice

Filling:

2 tablespoons butter

4 tablespoons white sugar

1 teaspoon ground star anise

1/4 teaspoon ground cinnamon

1 teaspoon vanilla paste

1/2 cup confectioners' sugar

*Directions*

Heat the milk in a microwave safe bowl and transfer the warm milk to the bowl of a stand electric mixer. Add the granulated sugar and yeast, and mix to combine well. Cover and let it sit until the yeast is foamy.

Then, beat the butter on low speed. Fold in the egg and mix again. Add salt and flour. Add the orange juice and mix on medium speed until a soft dough forms.

Knead the dough on a lightly floured surface. Cover it loosely and let it sit in a warm place about 1 hour or until doubled in size. Then, spritz the bottom and sides of a baking pan with cooking oil (butter flavored).

Roll your dough out into a rectangle.

Spread 2 tablespoons of butter all over the dough. In a mixing dish, combine the white sugar, ground star anise, cinnamon, and vanilla; sprinkle evenly over the dough.

Then, roll up your dough to form a log. Cut into 6 equal rolls and place them in the parchment-lined Air Fryer basket.

Bake at 350 degrees for 12 minutes, turning them halfway through the cooking time. Dust with confectioners' sugar and enjoy!

# Coconut Cheesecake Bites

*(Ready in about 25 minutes + chilling time | Servings 8)*

**Per serving:** 415 Calories; 32.3g Fat; 26.4g Carbs; 6.8g Protein; 17.1g Sugars

## Ingredients

1 ½ cups Oreo cookies, crushed

4 ounces granulated sugar

4 tablespoons butter, softened

12 ounces cream cheese

4 ounces double cream

2 eggs, lightly whisked

1 teaspoon pure vanilla extract

1 teaspoon pure coconut extract

1 cup toasted coconut

## Directions

Start by preheating your Air Fryer to 350 degrees F.

Mix the crushed Oreos with sugar and butter; press the crust into silicone cupcake molds. Bake for 5 minutes and allow them to cool on wire racks.

Using an electric mixer, whip the cream cheese and double cream until fluffy; add one egg at a time and continue to beat until creamy. Finally, add the vanilla and coconut extract.

Pour the topping mixture on top of the crust. Bake at 320 degrees F for 13 to 15 minutes.

Afterwards, top with the toasted coconut. Allow the mini cheesecakes to chill in your refrigerator before serving. Bon appétit!

# OTHER AIR FRYER FAVORITES

## Scrambled Eggs with Spinach and Tomato

*(Ready in about 15 minutes | Servings 2)*

**Per serving:** 274 Calories; 23.2g Fat; 5.7g Carbs; 13.7g Protein; 2.6g Sugars

*Ingredients*

2 tablespoons olive oil, melted

4 eggs, whisked

5 ounces fresh spinach, chopped

1 medium-sized tomato, chopped

1 teaspoon fresh lemon juice

1/2 teaspoon coarse salt

1/2 teaspoon ground black pepper

1/2 cup of fresh basil, roughly chopped

*Directions*

Add the olive oil to an Air Fryer baking pan. Make sure to tilt the pan to spread the oil evenly. Simply combine the remaining ingredients, except for the basil leaves; whisk well until everything is well incorporated.

Cook in the preheated Air Fryer for 8 to 12 minutes at 280 degrees F. Garnish with fresh basil leaves. Serve warm with a dollop of sour cream if desired.

## Colby Potato Patties

*(Ready in about 15 minutes | Servings 8)*

**Per serving:** 291 Calories; 18.0g Fat; 23.7g Carbs; 9.3g Protein; 1.7g Sugars

*Ingredients*

2 pounds white potatoes, peeled and grated

1/2 cup scallions, finely chopped

1/2 teaspoon freshly ground black pepper, or more to taste

1 tablespoon fine sea salt

1/2 teaspoon hot paprika

2 cups Colby cheese, shredded

1/4 cup canola oil

1 cup crushed crackers

*Directions*

Firstly, boil the potatoes until fork tender. Drain, peel and mash your potatoes.

Thoroughly mix the mashed potatoes with scallions, pepper, salt, paprika, and cheese. Then, shape the balls using your hands. Now, flatten the balls to make the patties.

In a shallow bowl, mix canola oil with crushed crackers. Roll the patties over the crumb mixture. Next, cook your patties at 360 degrees F approximately 10 minutes, working in batches. Serve with tabasco mayo if desired. Bon appétit!

## Zesty Broccoli Bites with Hot Sauce

*(Ready in about 20 minutes | Servings 6)*

**Per serving:** 80 Calories; 3.8g Fat; 10.8g Carbs; 2.5g Protein; 6.6g Sugars

*Ingredients*

For the Broccoli Bites:

1 medium-sized head broccoli, broken into florets

1/2 teaspoon lemon zest, freshly grated

1/3 teaspoon fine sea salt

1/2 teaspoon hot paprika

1 teaspoon shallot powder

1 teaspoon porcini powder

1/2 teaspoon granulated garlic

1/3 teaspoon celery seeds

1 ½ tablespoons olive oil

For the Hot Sauce:

1/2 cup tomato sauce

3 tablespoons brown sugar

1 tablespoon balsamic vinegar

1/2 teaspoon ground allspice

### Directions

Toss all the ingredients for the broccoli bites in a mixing bowl, covering the broccoli florets on all sides.

Cook them in the preheated Air Fryer at 360 degrees for 13 to 15 minutes. In the meantime, mix all ingredients for the hot sauce.

Pause your Air Fryer, mix the broccoli with the prepared sauce and cook for further 3 minutes. Bon appétit!

## Sweet Corn and Kernel Fritters

*(Ready in about 20 minutes | Servings 4)*

**Per serving:** 275 Calories; 8.4g Fat; 40.5g Carbs; 15.7g Protein; 7.3g Sugars

### Ingredients

1 medium-sized carrot, grated

1 yellow onion, finely chopped

4 ounces canned sweet corn kernels, drained

1 teaspoon sea salt flakes

1 heaping tablespoon fresh cilantro, chopped

1 medium-sized egg, whisked

2 tablespoons plain milk

1 cup of Parmesan cheese, grated

1/4 cup of self-rising flour

1/3 teaspoon baking powder

1/3 teaspoon brown sugar

### Directions

Press down the grated carrot in the colander to remove excess liquid. Then, spread the grated carrot between several sheets of kitchen towels and pat it dry.

Then, mix the carrots with the remaining ingredients in the order listed above.

Roll 1 tablespoon of the mixture into a ball; gently flatten it using the back of a spoon or your hand. Now, repeat with the remaining ingredients.

Spitz the balls with a nonstick cooking oil. Cook in a single layer at 350 degrees for 8 to 11 minutes or until they're firm to touch in the center. Serve warm and enjoy!

## Gorgonzola Stuffed Mushrooms with Horseradish Mayo

*(Ready in about 15 minutes | Servings 5)*

**Per serving:** 210 Calories; 15.2g Fat; 13.6g Carbs; 7.6g Protein; 2.7g Sugars

### Ingredients

1/2 cup of breadcrumbs

2 cloves garlic, pressed

2 tablespoons fresh coriander, chopped

1/3 teaspoon kosher salt

1/2 teaspoon crushed red pepper flakes

1 ½ tablespoons olive oil

20 medium-sized mushrooms, cut off the stems

1/2 cup Gorgonzola cheese, grated

1/4 cup low-fat mayonnaise

1 teaspoon prepared horseradish, well-drained

1 tablespoon fresh parsley, finely chopped

### Directions

Mix the breadcrumbs together with the garlic, coriander, salt, red pepper, and the olive oil; mix to combine well.

Stuff the mushroom caps with the breadcrumb filling. Top with grated Gorgonzola.

Place the mushrooms in the Air Fryer grill pan and slide them into the machine. Grill them at

380 degrees F for 8 to 12 minutes or until the stuffing is warmed through.

Meanwhile, prepare the horseradish mayo by mixing the mayonnaise, horseradish and parsley. Serve with the warm fried mushrooms. Enjoy!

# Potato Appetizer with Garlic-Mayo Sauce

*(Ready in about 19 minutes | Servings 4)*

**Per serving:** 277 Calories; 7.2g Fat; 50g Carbs; 6g Protein; 1.7g Sugars

*Ingredients*

2 tablespoons vegetable oil of choice

Kosher salt and freshly ground black pepper, to taste

3 Russet potatoes, cut into wedges

**For the Dipping Sauce:**

2 teaspoons dried rosemary, crushed

3 garlic cloves, minced

1/3 teaspoon dried marjoram, crushed

1/4 cup sour cream

1/3 cup mayonnaise

*Directions*

Lightly grease your potatoes with a thin layer of vegetable oil. Season with salt and ground black pepper.

Arrange the seasoned potato wedges in an air fryer cooking basket. Bake at 395 degrees F for 15 minutes, shaking once or twice.

In the meantime, prepare the dipping sauce by mixing all the sauce ingredients. Serve the potatoes with the dipping sauce and enjoy!

# The Best Sweet Potato Fries Ever

*(Ready in about 20 minutes | Servings 4)*

**Per serving:** 180 Calories; 5.4g Fat; 31.8g Carbs; 1.8g Protein; 0.7g Sugars

*Ingredients*

1 1/2 tablespoons olive oil

1/2 teaspoon smoked cayenne pepper

3 sweet potatoes, peeled and cut into 1/4-inch long slices

1/2 teaspoon shallot powder

1/3 teaspoon freshly ground black pepper, or more to taste

3/4 teaspoon garlic salt

*Directions*

Firstly, preheat your air fryer to 360 degrees F. Then, add the sweet potatoes to a mixing dish; toss them with the other ingredients.

Cook the sweet potatoes approximately 14 minutes. Serve with a dipping sauce of choice.

# Spicy Cheesy Risotto Balls

*(Ready in about 26 minutes | Servings 4)*

**Per serving:** 176 Calories; 9.1g Fat; 16.9g Carbs; 4.7g Protein; 5.2g Sugars

*Ingredients*

3 ounces cooked rice

1 /2 cup roasted vegetable stock

1 egg, beaten

1 cup white mushrooms, finely chopped

1/2 cup seasoned breadcrumbs

3 garlic cloves, peeled and minced

1/2 yellow onion, finely chopped

1/3 teaspoon ground black pepper, or more to taste

1 ½ bell peppers, seeded minced

1/2 chipotle pepper, seeded and minced

1/2 tablespoon Colby cheese, grated

1 ½ tablespoons canola oil

Sea salt, to savor

*Directions*

Heat a saucepan over a moderate heat; now, heat the oil and sweat the garlic, onions, bell pepper and chipotle pepper until tender. Throw in the mushrooms and fry until they are fragrant and the liquid has almost evaporated.

Throw in the cooked rice and stock; boil for 18 minutes. Now, add the cheese and spices; mix to combine.

Allow the mixture to cool completely. Shape the risotto mixture into balls. Dip the risotto balls in the beaten egg; then, roll them over the breadcrumbs.

Air-fry risotto balls for 6 minutes at 400 degrees F. Serve with marinara sauce and enjoy!

## Easy Cheesy Broccoli

*(Ready in about 25 minutes | Servings 4)*
**Per serving:** 103 Calories; 9.1g Fat; 4.9g Carbs; 1.9g Protein; 1.2g Sugars

*Ingredients*

1/3 cup grated yellow cheese
1 large-sized head broccoli, stemmed and cut small florets
2 1/2 tablespoons canola oil
2 teaspoons dried rosemary
2 teaspoons dried basil
Salt and ground black pepper, to taste

*Directions*

Bring a medium pan filled with a lightly salted water to a boil. Then, boil the broccoli florets for about 3 minutes.

Then, drain the broccoli florets well; toss them with the canola oil, rosemary, basil, salt and black pepper.

Set your air fryer to 390 degrees F; arrange the seasoned broccoli in the cooking basket; set the timer for 17 minutes. Toss the broccoli halfway through the cooking process.

Serve warm topped with grated cheese and enjoy!

## Potato and Kale Croquettes

*(Ready in about 9 minutes | Servings 6)*
**Per serving:** 309 Calories; 6.9g Fat; 49.8g Carbs; 12.1g Protein; 2g Sugars

*Ingredients*

4 eggs, slightly beaten
1/3 cup flour
1/3 cup goat cheese, crumbled
1 ½ teaspoons fine sea salt
4 garlic cloves, minced
1 cup kale, steamed
1/3 cup breadcrumbs
1/3teaspoon red pepper flakes
3 potatoes, peeled and quartered
1/3 teaspoon dried dill weed

*Directions*

Firstly, boil the potatoes in salted water. Once the potatoes are cooked, mash them; add the kale, goat cheese, minced garlic, sea salt, red pepper flakes, dill and one egg; stir to combine well.

Now, roll the mixture to form small croquettes. Grab three shallow bowls. Place the flour in the first shallow bowl.

Beat the remaining 3 eggs in the second bowl. After that, throw the breadcrumbs into the third shallow bowl.

Dip each croquette in the flour; then, dip them in the eggs bowl; lastly, roll each croquette in the breadcrumbs.

Air fry at 335 degrees F for 7 minutes or until golden. Tate, adjust for seasonings and serve warm.

# Spicy Potato Wedges

*(Ready in about 23 minutes | Servings 4)*

**Per serving:** 288 Calories; 4.7g Fat; 44.5g Carbs; 5.4g Protein; 3.7g Sugars

*Ingredients*

1 ½ tablespoons melted butter

1 teaspoon dried parsley flakes

1 teaspoon ground coriander

1 teaspoon seasoned salt

3 large-sized red potatoes, cut into wedges

1/2 teaspoon chili powder

1/3 teaspoon garlic pepper

*Directions*

Dump the potato wedges into the air fryer cooking basket. Drizzle with melted butter and cook for 20 minutes at 380 degrees F. Make sure to shake them a couple of times during the cooking process.

Add the remaining ingredients; toss to coat potato wedges on all sides. Bon appétit!

# Family Favorite Stuffed Mushrooms

*(Ready in about 16 minutes | Servings 2)*

**Per serving:** 176 Calories; 14.7g Fat; 10.5g Carbs; 6g Protein; 4g Sugars

*Ingredients*

2 teaspoons cumin powder

4 garlic cloves, peeled and minced

1 small onion, peeled and chopped

2 tablespoons bran cereal, crushed

18 medium-sized white mushrooms

Fine sea salt and freshly ground black pepper, to your liking

A pinch ground allspice

2 tablespoons olive oil

*Directions*

First, clean the mushrooms; remove the middle stalks from the mushrooms to prepare the "shells". Grab a mixing dish and thoroughly combine the remaining items. Fill the mushrooms with the prepared mixture.

Cook the mushrooms at 345 degrees F heat for 12 minutes. Enjoy!

# Cheese and Chive Stuffed Chicken Rolls

*(Ready in about 20 minutes | Servings 6)*

**Per serving:** 311 Calories; 18.3g Fat; 1.3g Carbs; 33.4g Protein; 0.3 g Sugars

*Ingredients*

2 eggs, well-whisked

Tortilla chips, crushed

1 1/2 tablespoons extra-virgin olive oil

1 ½ tablespoons fresh chives, chopped

3 chicken breasts, halved lengthwise

1 ½ cup soft cheese

2 teaspoons sweet paprika

1/2 teaspoon whole grain mustard

1/2 teaspoon cumin powder

1/3 teaspoon fine sea salt

1/3 cup fresh cilantro, chopped

1/3 teaspoon freshly ground black pepper, or more to taste

*Directions*

Flatten out each piece of the chicken breast using a rolling pin. Then, grab three mixing dishes.

In the first one, combine the soft cheese with the cilantro, fresh chives, cumin, and mustard.

In another mixing dish, whisk the eggs together with the sweet paprika. In the third dish, combine the salt, black pepper, and crushed tortilla chips.

Spread the cheese mixture over each piece of chicken. Repeat with the remaining pieces of the chicken breasts; now, roll them up.

Coat each chicken roll with the whisked egg; dredge each chicken roll into the tortilla chips mixture. Lower the rolls onto the air fryer cooking basket. Drizzle extra-virgin olive oil over all rolls.

Air fry at 345 degrees F for 28 minutes, working in batches. Serve warm, garnished with sour cream if desired.

## Chicken Drumsticks with Ketchup-Lemon Sauce

*(Ready in about 20 minutes + marinating time | Servings 6)*

**Per serving:** 274 Calories; 12g Fat; 17.3g Carbs; 23.3g Protein; 16.2g Sugars

### Ingredients

3 tablespoons lemon juice

1 cup tomato ketchup

1 ½ tablespoons fresh rosemary, chopped

6 skin-on chicken drumsticks, boneless

1/2 teaspoon ground black pepper

2 teaspoons lemon zest, grated

1/3 cup honey

3 cloves garlic, minced

### Directions

Dump the chicken drumsticks into a mixing dish. Now, add the other items and give it a good stir; let it marinate overnight in your refrigerator.

Discard the marinade; roast the chicken legs in your air fryer at 375 degrees F for 22 minutes, turning once.

Now, add the marinade and cook an additional 6 minutes or until everything is warmed through.

## Creamed Cajun Chicken

*(Ready in about 10 minutes | Servings 6)*

**Per serving:** 400 Calories; 10.2g Fat; 48.2g Carbs; 27.3g Protein; 3.5g Sugars

### Ingredients

3 green onions, thinly sliced

½ tablespoon Cajun seasoning

1 ½ cup buttermilk

2 large-sized chicken breasts, cut into strips

1/2 teaspoon garlic powder

1 teaspoon salt

1 cup cornmeal mix

1 teaspoon shallot powder

1 ½ cup flour

1 teaspoon ground black pepper, or to taste

### Directions

Prepare three mixing bowls. Combine 1/2 cup of the plain flour together with the cornmeal and Cajun seasoning in your bowl. In another bowl, place the buttermilk.

Pour the remaining 1 cup of flour into the third bowl.

Sprinkle the chicken strips with all the seasonings. Then, dip each chicken strip in the 1 cup of flour, then in the buttermilk; finally, dredge them in the cornmeal mixture.

Cook the chicken strips in the air fryer baking pan for 16 minutes at 365 degrees F. Serve garnished with green onions. Bon appétit!

# Chive, Feta and Chicken Frittata

*(Ready in about 10 minutes | Servings 4)*

**Per serving:** 176 Calories; 7.7g Fat; 2.4g Carbs; 22.8g Protein; 1.5g Sugars

*Ingredients*

1/3 cup Feta cheese, crumbled

1 teaspoon dried rosemary

½ teaspoon brown sugar

2 tablespoons fish sauce

1 ½ cup cooked chicken breasts, boneless and shredded

1/2 teaspoon coriander sprig, finely chopped

3 medium-sized whisked eggs

1/3 teaspoon ground white pepper

1 cup fresh chives, chopped

1/2 teaspoon garlic paste

Fine sea salt, to taste

Nonstick cooking spray

*Directions*

Grab a baking dish that fit in your air fryer.

Lightly coat the inside of the baking dish with a nonstick cooking spray of choice. Stir in all ingredients, minus Feta cheese. Stir to combine well.

Set your machine to cook at 335 degrees for 8 minutes; check for doneness. Scatter crumbled Feta over the top and eat immediately!

# Grilled Chicken Tikka Masala

*(Ready in about 35 minutes + marinating time | Servings 4)*

**Per serving:** 319 Calories; 20.1g Fat; 1.9g Carbs; 30.5g Protein; 0.1g Sugars

*Ingredients*

1 teaspoon Tikka Masala

1 teaspoon fine sea salt

2 heaping teaspoons whole grain mustard

2 teaspoons coriander, ground

2 tablespoon olive oil

2 large-sized chicken breasts, skinless and halved lengthwise

2 teaspoons onion powder

1 ½ tablespoons cider vinegar

Basmati rice, steamed

1/3 teaspoon red pepper flakes, crushed

*Directions*

Preheat the air fryer to 335 degrees for 4 minutes. Toss your chicken together with the other ingredients, minus basmati rice. Let it stand at least 3 hours.

Cook for 25 minutes in your air fryer; check for doneness because the time depending on the size of the piece of chicken.

Serve immediately over warm basmati rice. Enjoy!

# Award Winning Breaded Chicken

*(Ready in about 10 minutes + marinating time | Servings 4)*

**Per serving:** 262 Calories; 14.9g Fat; 2.7g Carbs; 27.5g Protein; 0.3g Sugars

*Ingredients*

**For the Marinade:**

1 1/2 teaspoons olive oil

1 teaspoon red pepper flakes, crushed

1/3 teaspoon chicken bouillon granules

1/3 teaspoon shallot powder

1 1/2 tablespoons tamari soy sauce

1/3 teaspoon cumin powder

1 ½ tablespoons mayo

1 teaspoon kosher salt

**For the chicken:**

2 beaten eggs

Breadcrumbs

1 ½ chicken breasts, boneless and skinless

1 ½ tablespoons plain flour

**Directions**

Butterfly the chicken breasts, and then, marinate them for at least 55 minutes.

Coat the chicken with plain flour; then, coat with the beaten eggs; finally, roll them in the breadcrumbs.

Lightly grease the cooking basket. Air-fry the breaded chicken at 345 degrees F for 12 minutes, flipping them halfway.

## Cheese and Garlic Stuffed Chicken Breasts

*(Ready in about 20 minutes | Servings 2)*

**Per serving:** 424 Calories; 24.5g Fat; 7.5g Carbs; 43.4g Protein; 5.3g Sugars

**Ingredients**

1/2 cup Cottage cheese

2 eggs, beaten

2 medium-sized chicken breasts, halved

2 tablespoons fresh coriander, chopped

1teaspoon fine sea salt

Seasoned breadcrumbs

1/3teaspoon freshly ground black pepper, to savor

3 cloves garlic, finely minced

**Directions**

Firstly, flatten out the chicken breast using a meat tenderizer.

In a medium-sized mixing dish, combine the Cottage cheese with the garlic, coriander, salt, and black pepper.

Spread 1/3 of the mixture over the first chicken breast. Repeat with the remaining ingredients. Roll the chicken around the filling; make sure to secure with toothpicks.

Now, whisk the egg in a shallow bowl. In another shallow bowl, combine the salt, ground black pepper, and seasoned breadcrumbs.

Coat the chicken breasts with the whisked egg; now, roll them in the breadcrumbs.

Cook in the air fryer cooking basket at 365 degrees F for 22 minutes. Serve immediately.

## Dinner Avocado Chicken Sliders

*(Ready in about 10 minutes | Servings 4)*

**Per serving:** 321 Calories; 18.7g Fat; 15.8g Carbs; 23.5g Protein; 1.2g Sugars

**Ingredients**

½ pounds ground chicken meat

4 burger buns

1/2 cup Romaine lettuce, loosely packed

½ teaspoon dried parsley flakes

1/3 teaspoon mustard seeds

1 teaspoon onion powder

1 ripe fresh avocado, mashed

1 teaspoon garlic powder

1 ½ tablespoon extra-virgin olive oil

1 cloves garlic, minced

Nonstick cooking spray

Salt and cracked black pepper (peppercorns), to taste

**Directions**

Firstly, spritz an air fryer cooking basket with a nonstick cooking spray.

Mix ground chicken meat, mustard seeds, garlic powder, onion powder, parsley, salt, and black pepper until everything is thoroughly combined. Make sure not to overwork the meat to avoid tough chicken burgers.

Shape the meat mixture into patties and roll them in breadcrumbs; transfer your burgers to the prepared cooking basket. Brush the patties with the cooking spray.

Air-fry at 355 F for 9 minutes, working in batches. Slice burger buns into halves. In the meantime, combine olive oil with mashed avocado and pressed garlic.

To finish, lay Romaine lettuce and avocado spread on bun bottoms; now, add burgers and bun tops. Bon appétit!

# Peanut Butter and Chicken Bites

*(Ready in about 10 minutes | Servings 8)*

**Per serving:** 150 Calories; 9.7g Fat; 2.1g Carbs; 12.9g Protein; 1.6g Sugars

*Ingredients*

1 ½ tablespoons soy sauce

1/2 teaspoon smoked cayenne pepper

8 ounces soft cheese

1 1/2 tablespoons peanut butter

1/3 leftover chicken

1 teaspoon sea salt

32 wonton wrappers

1/3 teaspoon freshly cracked mixed peppercorns

1/2 tablespoon pear cider vinegar

*Directions*

Combine all of the above ingredients, minus the wonton wrappers, in a mixing dish.

Lay out the wrappers on a clean surface. Now, spread the wonton wrappers with the prepared chicken filling.

Fold the outside corners to the center over the filling; after that, roll up the wrappers tightly; you can moisten the edges with a little water.

Set the air fryer to cook at 360 degrees F. Air fry the rolls for 6 minutes, working in batches. Serve with marinara sauce. Bon appétit!

# Tangy Paprika Chicken

*(Ready in about 30 minutes | Servings 4)*

**Per serving:** 312 Calories; 17.6g Fat; 2.6g Carbs; 30.4g Protein; 1.2g Sugars

*Ingredients*

1 ½ tablespoons freshly squeezed lemon juice

2 small-sized chicken breasts, boneless

1/2 teaspoon ground cumin

1 teaspoon dry mustard powder

1 teaspoon paprika

2 teaspoons cup pear cider vinegar

1 tablespoon olive oil

2 garlic cloves, minced

Kosher salt and freshly ground mixed peppercorns, to savor

*Directions*

Warm the olive oil in a nonstick pan over a moderate flame. Sauté the garlic for just 1 minutes.

Remove your pan from the heat; add cider vinegar, lemon juice, paprika, cumin, mustard powder, kosher salt, and black pepper. Pour this paprika sauce into a baking dish.

Pat the chicken breasts dry; transfer them to the prepared sauce. Bake in the preheated air fryer for about 28 minutes at 335 degrees F; check for doneness using a thermometer or a fork.

Allow to rest for 8 to 9 minutes before slicing and serving. Serve with dressing.

# Super-Easy Chicken with Tomato Sauce

*(Ready in about 20 minutes + marinating time | Servings 4)*

**Per serving:** 377 Calories; 24.8g Fat; 6.5g Carbs; 31.6g Protein; 4.1g Sugars

*Ingredients*

1 tablespoon balsamic vinegar

½ teaspoon red pepper flakes, crushed

1 fresh garlic, roughly chopped

2 ½ large-sized chicken breasts, cut into halves

1/3 handful fresh cilantro, roughly chopped

2 tablespoons olive oil

4 Roma tomatoes, diced

1 ½ tablespoons butter

1/3 handful fresh basil, loosely packed, sniped

1 teaspoon kosher salt

2 cloves garlic, minced

Cooked bucatini, to serve

### Directions

Place the first seven ingredients in a medium-sized bowl; let it marinate for a couple of hours.

Preheat the air fryer to 325 degrees F. Air-fry your chicken for 32 minutes and serve warm.

In the meantime, prepare the tomato sauce by preheating a deep saucepan. Simmer the tomatoes until you make a chunky mixture. Throw in the garlic, basil, and butter; give it a good stir.

Serve the cooked chicken breasts with the tomato sauce and the cooked bucatini. Bon appétit!

## Cheesy Pasilla Turkey

*(Ready in about 30 minutes | Servings 2)*

**Per serving:** 259 Calories; 19.1g Fat; 7.6g Carbs; 14g Protein; 1.5g Sugars

### Ingredients

1/3 cup Parmesan cheese, shredded

2 turkey breasts, cut into four pieces

1/3 cup mayonnaise

1 ½ tablespoons sour cream

1/2 cup crushed crackers

1 dried Pasilla peppers

1 teaspoon onion salt

1/3 teaspoon mixed peppercorns, freshly cracked

### Directions

In a shallow bowl, mix the crushed crackers, Parmesan cheese, onion salt, and the cracked mixed peppercorns together.

In a food processor, blitz the mayonnaise, along with the cream and dried Pasilla peppers until there are no lumps.

Coat the turkey breasts with this mixture, ensuring that all sides are covered.

Then, coat each piece of turkey in the Parmesan/cracker mix.

Now, preheat the air fryer to 365 degrees F; cook for 28 minutes until thoroughly cooked.

## Festive Turkey Drumsticks with Gala Apples

*(Ready in about 30 minutes + marinating time | Servings 6)*

**Per serving:** 100 Calories; 3.6g Fat; 14.7g Carbs; 4.9g Protein; 10.4g Sugars

### Ingredients

3 Gala apples, cored and diced

1/2 tablespoon Dijon mustard

2 sprigs rosemary, chopped

3 turkey drumsticks

1/3 cup cider vinegar

2 teaspoons olive oil

1/2cup tamari sauce

1/2 teaspoon smoked cayenne pepper

Kosher salt and ground black pepper, to taste

### Directions

Dump drumsticks, along with cider vinegar, tamari, and olive oil, into a mixing dish. Let it marinate overnight or at least 3 hours.

Set your air fryer to cook at 355 degrees F. Spread turkey drumsticks with Dijon mustard.

Season turkey drumsticks with salt, black pepper, smoked cayenne pepper, and rosemary;

Place the prepared drumstick in a lightly greased baking dish; scatter diced apples over them; work in batches, one drumstick at a time.

Pause the machine after 13 minutes; flip turkey drumstick and continue to cook for a further 10 minutes. Bon appétit!

# Roasted Turkey Sausage with Potatoes

*(Ready in about 40 minutes | Servings 6)*

**Per serving:** 212 Calories; 17.1g Fat; 6.3g Carbs; 8g Protein; 0.5g Sugars

### Ingredients

1/2 pound red potatoes, peeled and diced

1/2 teaspoon onion salt

1/2 teaspoon dried sage

1/2pound ground turkey

1/3 teaspoon ginger, ground

1 sprig rosemary, chopped

1 ½ tablespoons olive oil

1/2 teaspoon paprika

2 sprigs thyme, chopped

1 teaspoon ground black pepper

### Directions

In a bowl, mix the first six ingredients; give it a good stir. Heat a thin layer of vegetable oil in a nonstick skillet that is placed over a moderate flame.

Form the mixture into patties; fry until they're browned on all sides, or about 12 minutes.

Arrange the potatoes at the bottom of a baking dish. Sprinkle with the rosemary and thyme; add a drizzle of olive oil. Top with the turkey.

Roast for 32 minutes at 365 degrees F, turning once halfway through. Eat warm.

# Dinner Turkey Sandwiches

*(Ready in about 4 hours 30 minutes | Servings 4)*

**Per serving:** 114 Calories; 5.6g Fat; 3.6g Carbs; 13.1g Protein; 0.2g Sugars

### Ingredients

1/2 pound turkey breast

1 teaspoon garlic powder

7 ounces condensed cream of onion soup

1/3 teaspoon ground allspice

BBQ sauce, to savor

### Directions

Simply dump the cream of onion soup and turkey breast into your crock-pot. Cook on HIGH heat setting for 3 hours.

Then, shred the meat and transfer to a lightly greased baking dish.

Pour in your favorite BBQ sauce. Sprinkle with ground allspice and garlic powder. Air-fry an additional 28 minutes.

To finish, assemble the sandwiches; add toppings such as pickled or fresh salad, mustard, etc.

# Dijon and Curry Turkey Cutlets

*(Ready in about 30 minutes + marinating time | Servings 4)*

**Per serving:** 190 Calories; 16.8g Fat; 2.5g Carbs; 7.4g Protein; 0.8g Sugars

### Ingredients

1/2 tablespoon Dijon mustard

1/2 teaspoon curry powder

Sea salt flakes and freshly cracked black peppercorns, to savor

1/3pound turkey cutlets

1/2 cup fresh lemon juice

1/2 tablespoons tamari sauce

### Directions

Set the air fryer to cook at 375 degrees. Then, put the turkey cutlets into a mixing dish; add fresh lemon juice, tamari, and mustard; let it marinate at least 2 hours.

Coat each turkey cutlet with the curry powder, salt, and freshly cracked black peppercorns; roast for 28 minutes; work in batches. Bon appétit!

# Super Easy Sage and Lime Wings

*(Ready in about 30 minutes + marinating time | Servings 4)*

**Per serving:** 127 Calories; 7.6g Fat; 3.7g Carbs; 11.9g Protein; 0.2g Sugars

### Ingredients

1 teaspoon onion powder

1/3 cup fresh lime juice

1/2 tablespoon corn flour

1/2 heaping tablespoon fresh chopped parsley

1/3 teaspoon mustard powder

1/2 pound turkey wings, cut into smaller pieces

2 heaping tablespoons fresh chopped sage

1/2 teaspoon garlic powder

1/2 teaspoon seasoned salt

1 teaspoon freshly cracked black or white peppercorns

### Directions

Simply dump all of the above ingredients into a mixing dish; cover and let it marinate for about 1 hours in your refrigerator.

Air-fry turkey wings for 28 minutes at 355 degrees F. Bon appétit!

# Creamy Lemon Turkey

*(Ready in about 2 hours 25 minutes | Servings 4)*

**Per serving:** 260 Calories; 15.3g Fat; 8.9g Carbs; 28.6g Protein; 1.9g Sugars

### Ingredients

1/3 cup sour cream

2 cloves garlic, finely minced

1/3 teaspoon lemon zest

2 small-sized turkey breasts, skinless and cubed

1/3 cup thickened cream

2 tablespoons lemon juice

1 teaspoon fresh marjoram, chopped

Salt and freshly cracked mixed peppercorns, to taste

1/2 cup scallion, chopped

1/2 can tomatoes, diced

1 ½ tablespoons canola oil

### Directions

Firstly, pat dry the turkey breast. Mix the remaining items; marinate the turkey for 2 hours. Set the air fryer to cook at 355 degrees F. Brush the turkey with a nonstick spray; cook for 23 minutes, turning once. Serve with naan and enjoy!

# Turkey Wontons with Garlic-Parmesan Sauce

*(Ready in about 15 minutes | Servings 8)*

**Per serving:** 362 Calories; 13.5g Fat; 40.4g Carbs; 18.5g Protein; 1.2g Sugars

### Ingredients

8 ounces cooked turkey breasts, shredded

16 wonton wrappers

1 ½ tablespoons butter, melted

1/3 cup cream cheese, room temperature

8 ounces Asiago cheese, shredded

3 tablespoons Parmesan cheese, grated

1 teaspoon garlic powder

Fine sea salt and freshly ground black pepper, to taste

### Directions

In a small-sized bowl, mix the butter, Parmesan, garlic powder, salt, and black pepper; give it a good stir.

Lightly grease a mini muffin pan; lay 1 wonton wrapper in each mini muffin cup. Fill each cup with the cream cheese and turkey mixture.

Air-fry for 8 minutes at 335 degrees F. Immediately top with Asiago cheese and serve warm. Bon appétit!

# Cajun Turkey Meatloaf

*(Ready in about 45 minutes | Servings 6)*
**Per serving:** 429 Calories; 31.6g Fat; 8.3g Carbs; 25.3g Protein; 2.2g Sugars

*Ingredients*
1 1/3 pounds turkey breasts, ground
½ cup vegetable stock
2 eggs, lightly beaten
1/2 sprig thyme, chopped
1/2 teaspoon Cajun seasonings
1/2 sprig coriander, chopped
½ cup seasoned breadcrumbs
2 tablespoons butter, room temperature
1/2 cup scallions, chopped
1/3 teaspoon ground nutmeg
1/3 cup tomato ketchup
1/2 teaspoon table salt
2 teaspoons whole grain mustard
1/3 teaspoon mixed peppercorns, freshly cracked

*Directions*
Firstly, warm the butter in a medium-sized saucepan that is placed over a moderate heat; sauté the scallions together with the chopped thyme and coriander leaves until just tender.

While the scallions are sautéing, set your air fryer to cook at 365 degrees F.

Combine all the ingredients, minus the ketchup, in a mixing dish; fold in the sautéed mixture and mix again.

Shape into a meatloaf and top with the tomato ketchup. Air-fry for 50 minutes. Bon appétit!

# Wine-Braised Turkey Breasts

*(Ready in about 30 minutes + marinating time | Servings 4)*
**Per serving:** 230 Calories; 11.6g Fat; 15.2g Carbs; 16.1g Protein; 2.2g Sugars

*Ingredients*
1/3 cup dry white wine
1½ tablespoon sesame oil
1/2 pound turkey breasts, boneless, skinless and sliced
1/2 tablespoon honey
1/2 cup plain flour
2 tablespoons oyster sauce
Sea salt flakes and cracked black peppercorns, to taste

*Directions*
Set the air fryer to cook at 385 degrees. Pat the turkey slices dry and season with the sea salt flakes and the cracked peppercorns.

In a bowl, mix the other ingredients together, minus the flour; rub your turkey with this mixture. Set aside to marinate for at least 55 minutes.

Coat each turkey slice with the plain flour. Cook for 27 minutes; make sure to flip once or twice and work in batches. Bon appétit!

# Peppery Roasted Potatoes with Smoked Bacon

*(Ready in about 15 minutes | Servings 2)*
**Per serving:** 242 Calories; 11.6g Fat; 15,4g Carbs; 14.9g Protein; 5.7g Sugars

*Ingredients*
5 small rashers smoked bacon
1/3 teaspoon garlic powder
1 teaspoon sea salt
2 teaspoons paprika
1/3 teaspoon ground black pepper
1 bell pepper, seeded and sliced
1 teaspoon mustard
2 habanero peppers, halved

*Directions*
Simply toss all the ingredients in a mixing dish; then, transfer them to your air fryer's basket.
Air-fry at 375 degrees F for 10 minutes. Serve warm.

# Cornbread with Pulled Pork

*(Ready in about 24 minutes | Servings 2)*
**Per serving:** 239 Calories; 7.6g Fat; 6.3g Carbs; 34.6g Protein; 4g Sugars

*Ingredients*
2 ½ cups pulled pork, leftover works well too
1 teaspoon dried rosemary
1/2 teaspoon chili powder
3 cloves garlic, peeled and pressed
1/2 recipe cornbread
1/2 tablespoon brown sugar
1/3 cup scallions, thinly sliced
1 teaspoon sea salt

*Directions*
Preheat a large-sized nonstick skillet over medium heat; now, cook the scallions together with the garlic and pulled pork.

Next, add the sugar, chili powder, rosemary, and salt. Cook, stirring occasionally, until the mixture is thickened.
Preheat your air fryer to 335 degrees F. Now, coat two mini loaf pans with a cooking spray. Add the pulled pork mixture and spread over the bottom using a spatula.
Spread the previously prepared cornbread batter over top of the spiced pulled pork mixture.
Bake this cornbread in the preheated air fryer until a tester inserted into the center of it comes out clean, or for 18 minutes. Bon appétit!

# Famous Cheese and Bacon Rolls

*(Ready in about 10 minutes | Servings 6)*
**Per serving:** 386 Calories; 16.2g Fat; 29.7g Carbs; 14.7g Protein; 4g Sugars

*Ingredients*
1/3 cup Swiss cheese, shredded
10 slices of bacon
10 ounces canned crescent rolls
2 tablespoons yellow mustard 6

*Directions*
Start by preheating your air fryer to 325 degrees F.
Then, form the crescent rolls into "sheets". Spread mustard over the sheets. Place the chopped Swiss cheese and bacon in the middle of each dough sheet.
Create the rolls and bake them for about 9 minutes.
Then, set the machine to 385 degrees F; bake for an additional 4 minutes in the preheated air fryer.
Eat warm with some extra yellow mustard.

# Baked Eggs with Kale and Ham

*(Ready in about 15 minutes | Servings 2)*

**Per serving:** 417 Calories; 17.8g Fat; 3g Carbs; 61g Protein; 0.9g Sugars

*Ingredients*

2 eggs

1/4 teaspoon dried or fresh marjoram

2 teaspoons chili powder

1/3 teaspoon kosher salt

½ cup steamed kale

1/4 teaspoon dried or fresh rosemary

4 pork ham slices

1/3 teaspoon ground black pepper, or more to taste

*Directions*

Divide the kale and ham among 2 ramekins; crack an egg into each ramekin. Sprinkle with seasonings.

Cook for 15 minutes at 335 degrees F or until your eggs reach desired texture.

Serve warm with spicy tomato ketchup and pickles. Bon appétit!

# Easiest Pork Chops Ever

*(Ready in about 22 minutes | Servings 6)*

**Per serving:** 398 Calories; 21g Fat; 4.7g Carbs; 44.2g Protein; 0.5g Sugars

*Ingredients*

1/3 cup Italian breadcrumbs

Roughly chopped fresh cilantro, to taste

2 teaspoons Cajun seasonings

Nonstick cooking spray

2 eggs, beaten

3 tablespoons white flour

1 teaspoon seasoned salt

Garlic & onion spice blend, to taste

6 pork chops

1/3 teaspoon freshly cracked black pepper

*Directions*

Coat the pork chops with Cajun seasonings, salt, pepper, and the spice blend on all sides.

Then, add the flour to a plate. In a shallow dish, whisk the egg until pale and smooth. Place the Italian breadcrumbs in the third bowl.

Dredge each pork piece in the flour; then, coat them with the egg; finally, coat them with the breadcrumbs. Spritz them with cooking spray on both sides.

Now, air-fry pork chops for about 18 minutes at 345 degrees F; make sure to taste for doneness after first 12 minutes of cooking. Lastly, garnish with fresh cilantro. Bon appétit!

# Onion Rings Wrapped in Bacon

*(Ready in about 25 minutes | Servings 4)*

**Per serving:** 317 Calories; 16.8g Fat; 22.7g Carbs; 20.2g Protein; 2.7g Sugars

*Ingredients*

12 rashers back bacon

1/2 teaspoon ground black pepper

Chopped fresh parsley, to taste

1/2 teaspoon paprika

1/2 teaspoon chili powder

1/2 tablespoon soy sauce

½ teaspoon salt

*Directions*

Start by preheating your air fryer to 355 degrees F.

Season the onion rings with paprika, salt, black pepper, and chili powder. Simply wrap the bacon around the onion rings; drizzle with soy sauce.

Bake for 17 minutes, garnish with fresh parsley and serve. Bon appétit!

# Easy Pork Burgers with Blue Cheese

*(Ready in about 44 minutes | Servings 6)*
**Per serving:** 383 Calories; 19.5g Fat; 24.7g Carbs; 25.7g Protein; 4g Sugars

*Ingredients*

1/3 cup blue cheese, crumbled

6 hamburger buns, toasted

2 teaspoons dried basil

1/3 teaspoon smoked paprika

1 pound ground pork

2 tablespoons tomato puree

2 small-sized onions, peeled and chopped

1/2 teaspoon ground black pepper

3 garlic cloves, minced

1 teaspoon fine sea salt

*Directions*

Start by preheating your air fryer to 385 degrees F.

In a mixing dish, combine the pork, onion, garlic, tomato puree, and seasonings; mix to combine well.

Form the pork mixture into six patties; cook the burgers for 23 minutes. Pause the machine, turn the temperature to 365 degrees F and cook for 18 more minutes.

Place the prepared burger on the bottom bun; top with blue cheese; assemble the burgers and serve warm.

# Sausage, Pepper and Fontina Frittata

*(Ready in about 14 minutes | Servings 5)*
**Per serving:** 420 Calories; 19.6g Fat; 3.7g Carbs; 41g Protein; 2g Sugars

*Ingredients*

3 pork sausages, chopped

5 well-beaten eggs

1 ½ bell peppers, seeded and chopped

1 teaspoon smoked cayenne pepper

2 tablespoons Fontina cheese

1/2 teaspoon tarragon

1/2 teaspoon ground black pepper

1 teaspoon salt

*Directions*

In a cast-iron skillet, sweat the bell peppers together with the chopped pork sausages until the peppers are fragrant and the sausage begins to release liquid.

Lightly grease the inside of a baking dish with pan spray.

Throw all of the above ingredients into the prepared baking dish, including the sautéed mixture; stir to combine.

Bake at 345 degrees F approximately 9 minutes. Serve right away with the salad of choice.

# Country-Style Pork Meatloaf

*(Ready in about 25 minutes | Servings 4)*
**Per serving:** 460 Calories; 26.6g Fat; 3.9g Carbs; 48.9g Protein; 2g Sugars

*Ingredients*

1/2 pound lean minced pork

1/3 cup breadcrumbs

1/2 tablespoons minced green garlic

1½ tablespoon fresh cilantro, minced

1/2 tablespoon fish sauce

1/3 teaspoon dried basil

2 leeks, chopped

2 tablespoons tomato puree

1/2 teaspoons dried thyme

Salt and ground black pepper, to taste

*Directions*

Add all ingredients, except for breadcrumbs, to a large-sized mixing dish and combine everything using your hands.

Lastly, add the breadcrumbs to form a meatloaf. Bake for 23 minutes at 365 degrees F. Afterward, allow your meatloaf to rest for 10 minutes before slicing and serving. Bon appétit!

## Grilled Lemony Pork Chops

*(Ready in about 34 minutes | Servings 5)*
**Per serving:** 400 Calories; 23g Fat; 4.1g Carbs; 40.5g Protein; 1.5g Sugars

*Ingredients*

5 pork chops
1/3 cup vermouth
1/2 teaspoon paprika
2 sprigs thyme, only leaves, crushed
1/2 teaspoon dried oregano
Fresh parsley, to serve
1 teaspoon garlic salt½ lemon, cut into wedges
1 teaspoon freshly cracked black pepper
3 tablespoons lemon juice
3 cloves garlic, minced
2 tablespoons canola oil

*Directions*

Firstly, heat the canola oil in a sauté pan over a moderate heat. Now, sweat the garlic until just fragrant.

Remove the pan from the heat and pour in the lemon juice and vermouth. Now, throw in the seasonings. Dump the sauce into a baking dish, along with the pork chops.

Tuck the lemon wedges among the pork chops and air-fry for 27 minutes at 345 degrees F. Bon appétit!

## Herbed Crumbed Filet Mignon

*(Ready in about 20 minutes | Servings 4)*

**Per serving:** 268 Calories; 14.5g Fat; 1.0g Carbs; 32.0g Protein; 0.0g Sugars

*Ingredients*

1/2 pound filet mignon
Sea salt and ground black pepper, to your liking
1/2 teaspoon cayenne pepper
1 teaspoon dried basil
1 teaspoon dried rosemary
1 teaspoon dried thyme
1 tablespoon sesame oil
1 small-sized egg, well-whisked
1/2 cup seasoned breadcrumbs

*Directions*

Season the filet mignon with salt, black pepper, cayenne pepper, basil, rosemary, and thyme. Brush with sesame oil.

Put the egg in a shallow plate. Now, place the breadcrumbs in another plate.

Coat the filet mignon with the egg; then, lay it into the crumbs. Set your Air Fryer to cook at 360 degrees F.

Cook for 10 to 13 minutes or until golden. Serve with mixed salad leaves and enjoy!

## The Best London Broil Ever

*(Ready in about 30 minutes + marinating time | Servings 8)*
**Per serving:** 257 Calories; 9.2g Fat; 0.1g Carbs; 41.0g Protein; 0.4g Sugars

*Ingredients*

2 pounds London broil
3 large garlic cloves, minced
3 tablespoons balsamic vinegar
3 tablespoons whole-grain mustard
2 tablespoons olive oil
Sea salt and ground black pepper, to taste
1/2 teaspoon dried hot red pepper flakes

*Directions*

Score both sides of the cleaned London broil. Thoroughly combine the remaining ingredients; massage this mixture into the meat to coat it on all sides. Let it marinate for at least 3 hours.

Set the Air Fryer to cook at 400 degrees F; Then cook the London broil for 15 minutes. Flip it over and cook another 10 to 12 minutes. Bon appétit!

## Old-Fashioned Beef Stroganoff

*(Ready in about 20 minutes | Servings 4)*

**Per serving:** 352 Calories; 20.8g Fat; 10.0g Carbs; 29.8g Protein; 1.4g Sugars

*Ingredients*

3/4 pound beef sirloin steak, cut into small-sized strips

1/4 cup balsamic vinegar

1 tablespoon brown mustard

2 tablespoons all-purpose flour

1 tablespoon butter

1 cup beef broth

1 cup leek, chopped

2 cloves garlic, crushed

1 teaspoon cayenne pepper

Sea salt flakes and crushed red pepper, to taste

1 cup sour cream

2 ½ tablespoons tomato paste

*Directions*

Place the beef along with the balsamic vinegar and the mustard in a mixing dish; cover and marinate in your refrigerator for about 1 hour.

Then, coat the beef strips with the flour; butter the inside of a baking dish and put the beef into the dish.

Add the broth, leeks and garlic. Cook at 380 degrees for 8 minutes. Pause the machine and add the cayenne pepper, salt, red pepper, sour cream and tomato paste; cook for additional 7 minutes.

Check for doneness and serve with warm egg noodles, if desired. Bon appétit!

## Tender Beef Chuck with Brussels Sprouts

*(Ready in about 25 minutes + marinating time | Servings 4)*

**Per serving:** 302 Calories; 14.2g Fat; 6.5g Carbs; 36.6g Protein; 1.6g Sugars

*Ingredients*

1 pound beef chuck shoulder steak

2 tablespoons vegetable oil

1 tablespoon red wine vinegar

1 teaspoon fine sea salt

1/2 teaspoon ground black pepper

1 teaspoon smoked paprika

1 teaspoon onion powder

1/2 teaspoon garlic powder

1/2 pound Brussels sprouts, cleaned and halved

1/2 teaspoon fennel seeds

1 teaspoon dried basil

1 teaspoon dried sage

*Directions*

Firstly, marinate the beef with vegetable oil, wine vinegar, salt, black pepper, paprika, onion powder, and garlic powder. Rub the marinade into the meat and let it stay at least for 3 hours.

Air fry at 390 degrees F for 10 minutes. Pause the machine and add the prepared Brussels sprouts; sprinkle them with fennel seeds, basil, and sage.

Turn the machine to 380 degrees F; press the power button and cook for 5 more minutes. Pause the machine, stir and cook for further 10 minutes.

Next, remove the meat from the cooking basket and cook the vegetables a few minutes more if needed and according to your taste. Serve with your favorite mayo sauce.

# All-In-One Spicy Spaghetti with Beef

*(Ready in about 30 minutes | Servings 4)*

**Per serving:** 359 Calories; 5.5g Fat; 59.9g Carbs; 16.9g Protein; 2.7g Sugars

*Ingredients*

3/4 pound ground chuck

1 onion, peeled and finely chopped

1 teaspoon garlic paste

1 bell pepper, chopped

1 small-sized habanero pepper, deveined and finely minced

1/2 teaspoon dried rosemary

1/2 teaspoon dried marjoram

1 ¼ cups crushed tomatoes, fresh or canned

1/2 teaspoon sea salt flakes

1/4 teaspoon ground black pepper, or more to taste

1 package cooked spaghetti, to serve

*Directions*

In the Air Fryer baking dish, place the ground meat, onion, garlic paste, bell pepper, habanero pepper, rosemary, and the marjoram.

Air-fry, uncovered, for 10 to 11 minutes. Next step, stir in the tomatoes along with salt and pepper; cook 17 to 20 minutes. Serve over cooked spaghetti. Bon appétit!

# Beer-Braised Short Loin

*(Ready in about 15 minutes | Servings 4)*

**Per serving:** 379 Calories; 16.4g Fat; 3.7g Carbs; 46.0g Protein; 0.0g Sugars

*Ingredients*

1 ½ pounds short loin

2 tablespoons olive oil

1 bottle beer

2-3 cloves garlic, finely minced

2 Turkish bay leaves

*Directions*

Pat the beef dry; then, tenderize the beef with a meat mallet to soften the fibers. Place it in a large-sized mixing dish.

Add the remaining ingredients; toss to coat well and let it marinate for at least 1 hour.

Cook about 7 minutes at 395 degrees F; after that, pause the Air Fryer. Flip the meat over and cook for another 8 minutes, or until it's done.

# Beef and Kale Omelet

*(Ready in about 20 minutes | Servings 4)*

**Per serving:** 236 Calories; 13.7g Fat; 4.0g Carbs; 23.8g Protein; 1.0g Sugars

*Ingredients*

Non-stick cooking spray

1/2 pound leftover beef, coarsely chopped

2 garlic cloves, pressed

1 cup kale, torn into pieces and wilted

1 tomato, chopped

1/4 teaspoon brown sugar

4 eggs, beaten

4 tablespoons heavy cream

1/2 teaspoon turmeric powder

Salt and ground black pepper, to your liking

1/8 teaspoon ground allspice

*Directions*

Spritz the inside of four ramekins with a cooking spray.

Divide all of the above ingredients among the prepared ramekins. Stir until everything is well combined.

Air-fry at 360 degrees F for 16 minutes; check with a wooden stick and return the eggs to the Air Fryer for a few more minutes as needed. Serve immediately.

# RECIPE INDEX

Classic Pancakes with Blueberries 91
Cocktail Sausage and Veggies on a Stick 79
Coconut Cheesecake Bites 120
Coconut Pancake Cups 112
Colby Potato Patties 121
Corn on the Cob with Spicy Avocado Spread 97
Cornbread with Pulled Pork 134
Cornmeal Crusted Okra 95
Country-Style Pork and Mushroom Patties 33
Country-Style Pork Meatloaf 136
Couscous and Black Bean Bowl 89
Cracker Pork Chops with Mustard 31
Creamed Cajun Chicken 126
Creamed Trout Salad 58
Creamy Lemon Turkey 132
Crispy Parmesan Asparagus 75
Crispy Pork Wontons 92
Crispy Wax Beans with Almonds and Blue Cheese 68
Crunchy Asparagus with Mediterranean Aioli 84
Crunchy Roasted Chickpeas 83
Crunchy Roasted Pepitas 81
Crunchy Topped Fish Bake 58
Crusty Catfish with Sweet Potato Fries 57
Cube Steak with Cowboy Sauce 47

**D**
Delicious Asparagus and Mushroom Fritters 97
Delicious Coconut Granola 89
Delicious Sultana Muffins 86
Delicious Turkey Sandwiches 23
Dijon and Curry Turkey Cutlets 131
Dijon Ribs with Cherry Tomatoes 32
Dinner Avocado Chicken Sliders 128
Dinner Turkey Sandwiches 131
Double Cheese and Chicken Crescent Bake 25
Double Cheese Fish Casserole 61

**E**
Easiest Pork Chops Ever 135
Easy and Delicious Pizza Puffs 81
Easy Asian Gyudon 41
Easy Beef Jerky 45
Easy Cheesy Broccoli 124
Easy Chicken Sliders 16
Easy Creamy Shrimp Nachos 63
Easy Mexican Burritos 86
Easy Minty Meatballs 35
Easy Pork Burgers with Blue Cheese 136
Easy Thanksgiving Crunchwrap 25
Easy Vegan "Chicken" 101
Elegant Pork Chops with Applesauce 34
Enchilada Bake with Corn and Cheese 31
English-Style Scones with Raisins 109

**F**
Fall Harvest Apple Cinnamon Buns 116
Fall Vegetables with Spiced Yogurt 67
Family Favorite Stuffed Mushrooms 125
Family Vegetable Gratin 65
Famous Cheese and Bacon Rolls 134
Farmhouse Roast Turkey 17
Favorite New York Cheesecake 108
Festive Pork Fillets with Apples 32
Festive Turkey Drumsticks with Gala Apples 130
Filet of Flounder Cutlets 56
Filipino Pork Adobo 37
Filipino Tortang Giniling 43
Fried Asparagus with Goat Cheese 72
Fried Bread Pudding Squares 87
Fried Honey Banana 115

**G**
Golden Cornbread Muffins 88
Gorgonzola Stuffed Mushrooms with Horseradish Mayo 122
Greek Pork Loin with Tzatziki 38

Greek-Style Griddle Cakes 111
Greek-Style Roasted Vegetables 97
Green Bean Crisps 77
Grilled Banana Boats 108
Grilled Chicken Tikka Masala 127
Grilled Garlic and Avocado Toast 91
Grilled Hake with Garlic Sauce 53
Grilled Lemony Pork Chops 137
Grilled Tilapia with Portobello Mushrooms 53
Grilled Vienna Sausage with Broccoli 46

**H**
Halibut with Thai Lemongrass Marinade 59
Hawaiian Cheesy Meatball Sliders 33
Healthy Mac and Cheese 103
Herbed and Garlicky Pork Belly 29
Herbed Crumbed Filet Mignon 137
Homemade Apple Chips 83
Hungarian Mushroom Pilaf 99
Hungarian Oven Stew (Marha Pörkölt) 44

**I**
Indian Beef Samosas 46
Indian Malai Kofta 69
Italian Peperonata Classica 73
Italian Sausage Meatball Casserole 36
Italian-Style Crab Bruschetta 63
Italian-Style Tomato-Parmesan Crisps 76

**J**
Jamaican-Style Fish and Potato Fritters 60
Japanese Ribs (Supearibu no Nikomi) 34
Japanese Yaki Onigiri 93
Juicy Strip Steak 42

**K**
Kid-Friendly Vegetable Fritters 100
Kid-Friendly Veggie Tots 70
King Prawns with Lemon Butter Sauce 57
Korean Beef Bowl with Rice 41

**L**
Loaded Chicken Burgers 20
Loaded Tater Tot Bites 78

**M**
Marinated Chicken Drumettes with Asparagus 15
Marinated Tofu Bowl with Pearl Onions 101
Mashed Potatoes with Roasted Peppers 99
Meatloaf Muffins with Sweet Potato Frosting 34
Mediterranean Pita Pockets 91
Mediterranean-Style Potato Chips with Vegveeta Dip 105
Mexican Taco Bake 93
Mini Turkey and Corn Burritos 84
Minty Tender Filet Mignon 44
Mom's Orange Rolls 119
Mom's Toad in the Hole 51
Monkfish Fillets with Romano Cheese 53

**N**
Nana's Famous Apple Fritters 112
Nana's Turkey Chili 23

**O**
Old-Fashioned Beef Stroganoff 138
Old-Fashioned Plum Dumplings 117
Omelet with Prosciutto and Ricotta Cheese 36
Onion Rings with Spicy Ketchup 102
Onion Rings Wrapped in Bacon 135
Orange Glazed Scallops 59

**P**
Paprika Brussels Sprout Chips 106
Paprika Zucchini Bombs with Goat Cheese 82
Party Chicken Pillows 85
Party Greek Keftedes 78
Party Pork and Bacon Skewers 30
Pastrami and Cheddar Quiche 43
Peanut Butter and Chicken Bites 129

Super Easy Sage and Lime Wings 132
Super-Easy Chicken with Tomato Sauce 129
Sweet Corn and Kernel Fritters 122
Sweet Potato and Chickpea Tacos 70
Sweet-and-Sour Mixed Veggies 67
Swordfish with Roasted Peppers and Garlic
Sauce 55

**T**
Taco Casserole with Cheese 40
Tagliatelle al Ragu 37
Tangy Paprika Chicken 129
Tater Tot Vegetable Casserole 71
Tender Beef Chuck with Brussels Sprouts 138
Tex Mex Pasta Bake 95
The Best Chicken Burgers Ever 15
The Best Falafel Ever 101
The Best London Broil Ever 137
The Best Party Mix Ever 82
The Best Sweet Potato Fries Ever 123
Tofu and Brown Rice Bake 103
Traditional Chicken Teriyaki 20
Traditional Chicken Tetrazzini 24
Tuna Cake Burgers with Beer Cheese Sauce 63
Turkey and Sausage Meatloaf with Herbs 16
Turkey Breakfast Frittata 22

Turkey Wings with Butter Roasted Potatoes 17
Turkey Wontons with Garlic-Parmesan Sauce
132
Twice-Baked Potatoes with Pancetta 74
Tyrolean Kaiserschmarrn (Austrian Pancakes)
96

**U**
Ultimate Vegan Calzone 105

**V**
Vegetable Kabobs with Simple Peanut Sauce
106
Vermouth Bacon and Turkey Burgers 26

**W**
Warm Farro Salad with Roasted Tomatoes 98
White Chocolate Rum Molten Cake 118
Wine-Braised Turkey Breasts 133
Winter Bliss Bowl 71
Winter Squash and Tomato Bake 98
Winter Vegetable Braise 65

**Y**
Yakitori (Japanese Chicken Skewers) 80

**Z**
Zesty Broccoli Bites with Hot Sauce 121